PRINCIPLES OF PRAYER

PRINCIPLES OF PRAYER

by
Billy Joe Daugherty

Principles of Prayer
ISBN 1-56267-099-9
Copyright © 1996
Billy Joe Daugherty
Victory Christian Center
7700 South Lewis Avenue
Tulsa, OK 74136-7700
(918) 491-7700

Objectives of This Unit of Study

Some of the primary objectives of this unit of study are:

1.   To commit myself to a life of prayer.

2.   To accept Christ's righteousness for my unrighteousness, freeing me of fear, inferiority, guilt and condemnation, which are major hindrances to effective prayer.

3.   To accept Christ's grace, mercy and love and to loose these same qualities upon others in exchange for unforgiveness, resentment, bitterness, envy and other works of the flesh.

4.   To exercise the key to success in this life, which is a time of communion with the Lord in the Word and in prayer, before the start of each day.

5.   To pray in the Spirit as well as in my understanding, asking for interpretation of that which is prayed in the Spirit.

6.   To follow Jesus' example in prayer.

7.   To align my thoughts, words and motives with God's Word.

8.   To pray with accuracy according to God's Word.

9.   To discern the types of prayer that should be used in any particular situation.

10.   To incorporate the prayer of praise and thanksgiving with all kinds of prayer.

11.   To speak to the mountains of challenge in my life and see them removed.

12.   To mature spiritually through the development of an intimate prayer life based upon God's Word.

CONTENTS

INTRODUCTION

My primary motive for writing this book—based upon the principles of prayer found in God's Word—is to give you some sound guidelines for effective prayer, which is the backbone of a successful life and ministry.

Jesus' very life is an example of effective prayer. He was in continual communion with the Father. He spoke only what the Father spoke. You don't have to pitch one up there and hope someone upstairs catches it! You can pray with the same intimacy and accuracy that Jesus did if you will follow His example.

There are many types of prayer—the prayer of agreement, individual, united or corporate prayer, the prayer of commitment, prayer in the Spirit and in your understanding, the prayer of faith and the prayer of praise and thanksgiving—all of which are operational and strategic once you understand your own position of righteousness in Christ Jesus.

Prayer shouldn't be a drag. It should be the highlight of your day, starting with early morning prayer and keeping an ear to the Holy Spirit throughout the entire day.

Effective prayer will cause you to soar like an eagle in God's plans for you. It is the key to tapping into the wisdom of God, which will elevate you above mediocrity, cause you to excel in God's Kingdom, and perform the "great exploits" spoken of in Daniel 11:32 AMP:

> **But the people who know their God shall prove themselves strong and shall stand firm and do exploits [for God].**

Because of an intimate prayer life, you will be stable, secure and immovable in the work of the Lord, as Paul described in 1 Corinthians 15:58 AMP:

> **Therefore, my beloved brethren, be firm (steadfast), immovable, always abounding in the**

work of the Lord [always being superior, excelling, doing more than enough in the service of the Lord], knowing and being continually aware that your labor in the Lord is not futile [it is never wasted or to no purpose].

Even as world conditions become darker and darker, the light of Christ radiated through you will become brighter and brighter as you yield to the Holy Spirit and allow prayer to become an integral part of your life.

As God's children, it's time for us to become more like Jesus Christ, for one day soon **"we shall see Him just as He [really] is!"** (1 John 3:2 AMP).

Billy Joe Daugherty

The effectual fervent prayer
of a righteous man
availeth much.

James 5:16 KJV

CHAPTER 1
CALLED TO A LIFE OF PRAYER

> **Do not remember the former things, nor consider the things of old.**
>
> **Behold, I will do a new thing, now it shall spring forth; shall you not know it? I will even make a road in the wilderness and rivers in the desert...**
>
> **I, even I, am He who blots out your transgressions for My own sake; and I will not remember your sins.**
>
> **Isaiah 43:18,19,25**

Today is a new day! Regardless of your past prayer life, *now* is the time to start fresh in your spiritual walk, with prayer an integral part of it.

Your prayer life reveals how much you depend on God and how much you depend on yourself. Your prayer life is an indicator of where your trust lies.

God moves in this earth only in response to prayer. An example of this is when Dr. Lester Sumrall, as a young missionary, fell off of a mule while riding over the mountains of Tibet with a mule train. Because he was on the last mule in the group, no one even noticed when he became deathly ill and fell from his mule. Dr. Sumrall knew he was dying, and he lost consciousness.

After a few hours he awakened totally refreshed and healed. In the natural, it was impossible to know which one of the many trails to take, but he got back on the mule, and amazingly, the mule found the little village where the rest of the team spent the night.

A year later, when Dr. Sumrall was back in the states, he met with a little prayer warrior who opened up her diary and asked him what he was doing at a particular time. She had written in her diary when God awoke her to pray and said, "Lester Sumrall is dying. Pray." Because she was obedient to the Spirit of God to pray, Lester Sumrall's life was spared. Prayer can mean the difference between life and death. As Christians, we need to be consistent in prayer.

On October 22, 1991, when our house caught on fire, we later learned that many people were awakened by the Spirit of God between 1:30 and 2:00 that morning to pray for us. As one family was preparing for bed a few hours earlier, a spirit of intercession came on them and they prayed for us. In the natural, they had no way of knowing that we would face a crisis for our very lives less than four hours later.

The fire chief said that it was one of the worst smoke damaged homes he had ever seen in the city of Tulsa. Smoke blanketed everything in the areas that were not totally burned out. The fire chief ordered an extra truck with workers to be brought to the scene to recover the bodies because they did not expect anybody to get out alive. He said, "We could not believe that you all got out." Prayer makes a difference!

Later, when we walked back through the house, we realized we were probably only thirty seconds from death, but God brought us out. I believe our own prayers made a difference, but I also believe the prayers of other people made a difference. I will be grateful for those prayers forever.

Most people have had some narrow escapes—some they are aware of and some they're not aware of. When someone prays, God sends His angels for protection and deliverance.

In Daniel 10 when Daniel prayed, for twenty-one days there was seemingly no answer. An angel appeared to him and said, **"Do not fear, Daniel, for from the first day that you set your heart to understand, and to humble yourself before your God, your words were heard;** *and I have come because of your words"* (Daniel 10:12). *The King James Version* says, *"I am come for thy words."* God is moving in response to your words.

The battle in prayer is whether you are going to take the words of the world, the words of the circumstances, or the Word of God to Him in prayer. God's Word is alive, powerful and sharper than any two-edged sword, and He watches over His Word to perform it.

A few years ago, a pregnant woman came to Sharon for prayer after doctors gave her a diagnosis that the baby in her womb was dead. She had not felt movement for some time. Doctors were ready to perform an abortion. Sharon laid hands on her womb and prayed, then encouraged the woman to go to another doctor for a second examination and opinion.

After being examined again, doctors discovered that the child was alive. Today, Dan and Sue Hunt's little boy is a healthy, happy child. Prayer was the key that brought life into a situation that appeared to be devastating. God can work miracles if someone will pray. He will show you a way when there seems to be no way.

One of the ladies in our church shared a testimony with us of being in a Victory Christian Center service when we had a young man testify of praying for the salvation of a family member. As he led in prayer, that young man had people stand who were believing for the salvation of loved ones. This woman stood for the salvation of her sister. As the young man finished praying, he said, "Try to make contact this week with the people you stood for tonight."

When this woman got home that night, she called her sister. When her sister picked up the phone, she said, "Guess what? I got

3

saved at church tonight." Prayer that is in agreement with God's Word works!

Several years ago, Sharon and I were in an afternoon session at Christ For The Nations. A member of the student body was about to have a baby, and the position of the baby indicated that it would be born breach.

Freda Lindsay asked us to pray and agree that the baby would turn around because doctors were to make their decision within one hour whether to take the baby by Caesarean section.

Before the Sunday afternoon meeting was over, Mrs. Lindsay made the announcement that the baby had turned and was delivered healthy and normal. Hallelujah! God can turn your situations around if someone will pray.

Years ago one of our friends went to a large Southeastern Methodist Conference. A number of theologians were scheduled to speak on a panel. A charismatic Methodist pastor's wife lost the buckle on her shoe. As she walked down the hall, she was praying as she looked for it. One minister asked, "May I help you, Ma'am?" She said, "I am praying to find my shoe buckle." He didn't say anything, but he looked around and then walked on. He was one of the speakers on the panel.

As the panel talked about the subject of prayer, he related the incident of this woman looking for her shoe buckle. He said, "I can't believe that someone would bother God to find a shoe buckle." He actually belittled the woman from the podium.

Oral Roberts was on the same panel. When they gave him the microphone, he said, "God is concerned with everything that concerns you." God is big enough to take care of the little things. He is interested in the details of your life. He turned the water into wine at the wedding in Cana. He multiplied the loaves and fishes so the multitude wouldn't go home hungry.

God is concerned about the practical, personal things in your life; and if you don't pray about everything, you probably won't pray about anything!

Praying for Others

Every believer is called to a life of prayer. As you respond to the call to pray and you begin to pray for others, your own captivity will be turned. The law of sowing and reaping works in prayer as well as in finances.

Job 42:10 says, **"And the Lord restored Job's losses when he prayed for his friends. Indeed the Lord gave Job twice as much as he had before."** If you have needs, pray for someone else. As you give out, you will receive back into your own life.

In Psalm 2:8, God spoke to His Son and said, **"Ask of Me, and I will give You the nations for Your inheritance, and the ends of the earth for Your possession."** *The King James Version* of this verse says, **"Ask of me, and I shall give thee the heathen for thine inheritance, and the uttermost parts of the earth for thy possession."**

When you begin to move into the realm of prayer for others, your own needs will be met. You can touch every nation in the world through prayer.

Matthew 6:33 applies to prayer as well as to finances. **"But seek first the kingdom of God and His righteousness, and all these things shall be added to you."**

Prayer is interconnected with every area of your life. If you are living a prayerless life, you are fooling yourself, but you aren't fooling God and you certainly aren't fooling the devil. Without prayer, your life is open prey to the enemy. You will have to deal with him on your own turf. Without the power of prayer, you are no match for the devil. His schemes, plots and trickery go beyond your ability to resist, but with God on your side, who can stand against you?

You can't lose if you will stay hooked up with Jesus through a life that is committed to prayer.

Gospel Prayer Truths

Here are twelve gospel prayer truths from Chapter 1:

1. Your prayer life reveals how much you depend on God and how much you depend on yourself.

2. God moves in the earth in response to prayer.

3. Prayer can make the difference between life and death.

4. When someone prays, God sends His angels of protection and deliverance.

5. God moves in response to your words.

6. God works miracles when people pray.

7. Prayer that is in agreement with God's Word works.

8. God is concerned with everything—little and big—that concerns you.

9. You can pray about everything and anything.

10. Every believer is called to a life of prayer.

11. The law of sowing and reaping works in prayer as well as in finances.

12. Without prayer, your life is open prey to the devil.

QUESTIONS

Part 1. Completion

Please complete each of the statements.

1. Prayer can mean the difference between _____ and
   _____ .

2. Like Daniel, God moves in response to your _____
   (Daniel 10:12).

3. To be effective in prayer, you must speak _____
   _____ rather than the circumstances or the words
   of the world.

4. _____ is interconnected with every area of your
   life.

5. Without prayer, your life is open prey to the _____.

Part 2. Personal Application

Please complete the questions and/or statements to the best of
your ability.

1. I am facing a personal situation right now where I have an
   opportunity to believe the circumstances instead of believing
   God's Word. The situation is: _____

   _____

   _____

   _____

   The Scripture(s) I am believing and applying to this situation
   is (are): _____

   _____

   _____

   _____

2. I am also praying for another person's need, which is: _____

_____

_____

_____

The Scripture(s) I am believing and applying to this situation is (are):_____

_____

_____

_____

CHAPTER 2
AN UNDERSTANDING
OF RIGHTEOUSNESS

Prayer is communion with God where you speak to Him, you listen to Him and you hear from Him. Prayer is really an exchange of divine life and purpose. This is why it is so important to pray according to God's will. Since His will and His Word are one and the same, effective prayer is based upon praying the Word.

Many people can look back on their lives and realize the emptiness and fruitlessness they experienced at times, which was a result of a lack of prayer. Often, failure in an area of life is the result of failure to spend time in the Word and in prayer. People can blame circumstances, people and world conditions, but success in your life depends upon your prayer life. Prayer will change your circumstances. It will bring God on the scene. It will cause divine intervention to come on your behalf, which will reverse negative circumstances.

Cleanse Your Heart

The psalmist David said:

The eyes of the Lord are on the righteous, and His ears are open to their cry.

The face of the Lord is against those who do evil, to cut off the remembrance of them from the earth.

The righteous cry out, and the Lord hears, and delivers them out of all their troubles.

Psalm 34:15-17

Psalm 66:18 says:

If I regard iniquity in my heart, the Lord will not hear.

The Spirit of God spoke through the prophets numerous times indicating that sin will block God's blessings from reaching you. Therefore, the first thing you need to do to set the stage for effectual prayer is to cleanse your heart by repenting of sin. God hears the cry of a repentant sinner who asks for mercy and forgiveness. But for the person who knows about God, who knows about His standards of righteousness and refuses to let go of sin, his prayers will be short-circuited.

Romans 8:1 says, **"There is therefore now no condemnation to those who are in Christ Jesus...."** By faith, you are in Christ Jesus when you are born again. There is no condemnation to those **"who do not walk according to the flesh, but according to the Spirit."** There is no condemnation if you are in Christ Jesus *if you continue to walk in the Spirit rather than in the flesh, in obedience to God's laws.*

This same truth is repeated in 1 Peter 3:12:

For the eyes of the Lord are on the righteous, and His ears are open to their prayers; but the face of the Lord is against those who do evil.

This truth applies to those who are under the new covenant as well as to those who were under the old covenant.

First Peter 3:11 says:

Let him turn away from evil and do good; let him seek peace and pursue it.

The eyes of the Lord are over the righteous and His ears are open unto their prayers, but the face of the Lord is against those who do evil. Peter is talking about a lifestyle. He is talking about how a husband is to treat his wife and vice versa, and indicates that proper behavior will enhance the prayers of the marriage partners.

10

> **Husbands, likewise, dwell with them with under-
> standing, giving honor to the wife, as to the weaker
> vessel, and as being heirs together of the grace of
> life, that your prayers may not be hindered.**
>
> **1 Peter 3:7**

Peter is saying that the way you treat people, starting with
your own family members, will either hinder or enhance your
prayers.

Righteousness—A Requirement
for Effective Prayer

James 5:16 KJV says, **"The effectual fervent prayer of a
righteous man availeth much."** The term, *a righteous man,*
includes a righteous woman, a teenager, or a child. *The Amplified
Translation* of this verse says, **"The earnest (heartfelt, continued) prayer of a righteous man makes tremendous power
available [dynamic in its working]."** This verse in *The Living
Bible* says, **"The earnest prayer of a righteous man has great
power and wonderful results."**

The awesome power released through effectual prayer is
demonstrated in James 5:17,18:

> **Elijah was a man with a nature like ours, and
> he prayed earnestly that it would not rain; and it
> did not rain on the land for three years and six
> months.**
>
> **And he prayed again, and the heaven gave rain,
> and the earth produced its fruit.**

Elijah wasn't a superman! He was a human being. He faced
the same temptations you and I face yet he prayed earnestly. For
there to be no rain on the earth for three years and six months as
a result of Elijah's praying is potent prayer!

James draws a parallel. He was saying, "You are no different than Elijah. Elijah was a man with like passions as you have. He faced the same temptations you face." The point is, we can pray with the same effectiveness as Elijah.

The prayers of the saints can open or shut heaven. They can shut up natural forces. Elijah's prayers affected nature. Drought and famine came. Elijah wasn't praying out of a personal vendetta. What he prayed had a focused purpose, because God showed him that heaven was going to be shut for a season.

An intercessor hears from God and prays His will into the earth in a focused direction. There is a two-way communication. You talk and you listen. God reveals what He wants prayed into the earth. God needs human beings to bring His will to pass on the earth.

Why did Elijah's prayer have such a great effect? First, he was a righteous man. Second, he prayed according to God's will. Elijah was righteous by his faith. It wasn't that he didn't have human passions, challenges and temptations. At one point in his life, Elijah was ready to take his own life, running from Jezebel in fear.

You will have power in prayer when you know you are righteous. Some people have said, "I don't know if the Lord hears my prayers." If you know you are righteous, you can be assured that God hears your prayers. You don't have to wonder, "Did I pitch one up to the ceiling? How high did it get? Did it bounce back?" No! When you know you are righteous, you know God's ears are open to your prayers.

Knowing that you are *the righteousness of God in Christ is the absolute basis for effective prayer.* People of most religions pray, but it's not enough just to pray. You must pray accurately with knowledge, information and wisdom.

Romans 10:8-10 says:

But what does it say? "The word is near you, in your mouth and in your heart" (that is, the word

of faith which we preach): that if you confess with your mouth the Lord Jesus and believe in your heart that God has raised Him from the dead, you will be saved.

For with the heart one believes to righteousness, and with the mouth confession is made unto salvation.

We believe by faith that Jesus Christ's blood paid for our sins and that His death, burial and resurrection have granted us the free gift of righteousness. He took our sin, and He paid our penalty. Righteousness comes to us by faith in the complete work of the shed blood of Jesus Christ.

What will righteousness do for you? It will deliver you from fear, condemnation, inferiority and guilt. When you know you are in right standing with God, you know that He hears you. If He hears you, you can have confidence that your prayers will be answered when you pray according to His Word.

When you know that God is for you, He is with you and He is on your side, you don't have to be afraid of anything. Fear will leave you when you know you are right with God.

Romans 3:10 says, **"There is none righteous, no, not one."** Isaiah 64:6 says, **"All our righteousnesses are like filthy rags...."** It is obvious that none of us can be righteous by our own works.

In Romans 3, Paul was saying, "The law came, but it could not make people righteous. It didn't change their nature. It gave them a visible, outward, external picture of what God desired, but it couldn't change man on the inside." Paul went on to explain that righteousness comes by faith in Jesus Christ.

But now the righteousness of God apart from the law is revealed, being witnessed by the Law and the Prophets.

Romans 3:21

13

In other words, the law and the prophets foretold the need for righteousness. All the sacrifices indicated that we needed to be forgiven by shed blood. Everything that was done revealed that we had to have some type of salvation.

> **Even the righteousness of God, through faith in Jesus Christ, to all and on all who believe. For there is no difference.**
>
> **Romans 3:22**

This righteousness comes *by faith in Jesus Christ* to all who believe. It is available to the whole world, but it will only come upon those who believe in Jesus Christ.

When Paul says, **"For there is no difference,"** he was saying, There is no difference between the Jew and the Gentile, **"For all have sinned and fall short of the glory of God"** (Romans 3:23).

Many people use this verse as a hammer to beat people over the head, but when we read it in context, it gives a totally different viewpoint. Paul was saying, "Since we have all sinned, and Jesus paid for the sins of all, then all can be made righteous by faith in Jesus Christ."

> **Being justified freely by His grace through the redemption that is in Christ Jesus.**
>
> **Romans 3:24**

Being justified means "declared righteous." We have been acquitted. We have been found "not guilty," because Jesus Christ took our penalty. We were all guilty, but because of the completed work of Jesus Christ at Calvary, we have been justified.

The Judge of the Supreme Court of the Universe has taken the evidence—we were sinners—but Jesus Christ offered *His blood* for our sins. Our papers were stamped, "Not guilty. I forgive you, I pardon you and I declare that the righteousness of the One Who gave His blood is now yours. I will look at you the way I look at Him."

When God looks at you in your prayer life, He looks at you through the blood of His Son. When a slave is purchased, he is redeemed out of slavery and brought into freedom. We were bought, and the redemption price was the blood of Jesus Christ.

For God so loved the world that He gave His only begotten Son, that whoever believes in Him should not perish but have everlasting life [or total liberty for all eternity].

John 3:16

Whom God set forth as a propitiation [a sacrifice] **by His blood, through faith, to demonstrate His righteousness, because in His forbearance God had passed over the sins that were previously committed.**

Romans 3:25

Second Corinthians 5:21 says, **"For He made Him who knew no sin to be sin for us, that we might become the righteousness of God in Him."** Romans 5:17 says, **"Those who receive abundance of grace and of the gift of righteousness will reign in life through the One, Jesus Christ."** In other words, if you don't know you are righteous, then someone other than Christ is going to reign over you. Until you receive a revelation of righteousness, you will remain under your circumstances and under the rule of the devil.

There is a great difference between self-righteousness and the gift of righteousness. None of us are righteous in our own works, but all who believe can be righteous through the work of Jesus Christ. When God looks at us and we are forgiven, His eyes will be open to us and His ears will be open to our prayers. Then our prayers will be effective!

When you know you are the righteousness of God through faith in Jesus Christ, you will have Holy Ghost boldness in your prayer life.

Many people pray, but they have no confidence that their prayers are being heard. They have no confidence that they have access into the presence of the Father in Jesus' name. I have heard people say, "I pitched one up there. I hope the Big Man upstairs caught it!"

When you know who you are in Christ, you will pray with authority. When you have a revelation of your sonship—that you are a child of God and no longer an outcast, but accepted and loved as part of His family—your prayers will be effective.

When a person becomes a Christian, he becomes a brand-new person. Old things pass away and all things become new. Your spirit is made right with God. In other words, when Jesus washes your heart in His blood, He cleanses it completely.

You will reign in this life when you have confidence that your prayers are being heard and answered. Whatever you face, you will know that you have direct access to the Father and that He will hear you and move in your behalf. If He has to move heaven and earth, He will do it for you because you are in the family—His family!

You need to say, "By the blood of Jesus Christ and by the grace of God, I have received the gift of righteousness. I am now a child of God."

Hebrews 4:12-14 says:

> **For the word of God is living and powerful, and sharper than any two-edged sword, piercing even to the division of soul and spirit, and of joints and marrow, and is a discerner of the thoughts and intents of the heart.**
>
> **And there is no creature hidden from His sight, but all things are naked and open to the eyes of Him to whom we must give account.**
>
> **Seeing then that we have a great High Priest who has passed through the heavens, Jesus the Son of God, let us hold fast our confession.**

When Jesus passed into the heavens, He took His blood as our High Priest. In the Old Testament, once a year the high priest would go into the holy of holies with the blood of a sacrificial animal. That blood was sprinkled upon the mercy seat. But Hebrews 9 tells us that the blood of bulls and calves could not cleanse us and remove our sins. So Jesus Christ, the Great Shepherd, the High Priest, took His own blood into the holy of holies and made a once-and-for-all sacrifice for our sins.

In the Old Testament, the blood sacrifice of an animal by the high priest was an atonement or a covering. In the New Testament, the blood sacrifice of Jesus Christ totally remits or blots out our sins. Under the new covenant, the Lord said, **"For I will be merciful to their unrighteousness, and their sins and their lawless deeds I will remember no more"** (Hebrews 8:12).

Hebrews 4:15 KJV says:

> **For we have not an high priest which cannot be touched with the feeling of our infirmities; but was in all points tempted like as we are, yet without sin.**

Jesus is our High Priest, and He can identify with our problems. He is touched when we pray. He knows what we are going through, because He was tempted in all points like we are.

Hebrews 4:16 says:

> **Let us therefore *come boldly to the throne of grace*, that we may obtain mercy and find grace to help in time of need.**

We can come boldly and with confidence to the throne of grace in prayer, because we have been made righteous through the blood of Jesus Christ. We come to the Father in Jesus' name to obtain mercy and find grace to help any time we have a need in our lives.

When you understand the work of Jesus' blood, you will not approach the Father with fear, inferiority, condemnation, or guilt.

You will approach Him with boldness, speaking in line with His Word which is His will, refusing to be denied whether you are praying for yourself or for someone else.

Ephesians 2:13-18 gives us further revelation about the righteousness of God which we receive at the new birth through Christ in exchange for our sins. What an exchange!

But now in Christ Jesus you who once were far off have been brought near by the blood of Christ.

Ephesians 2:13

When you know that you are the righteousness of God, you no longer feel that you are at a distance or separated from God. That's why Scripture says, **"Come boldly to the throne of grace..."** (Hebrews 4:16).

I remember Ken Copeland sharing that early in his Christian walk, he prayed like he heard other people pray. "Oh, God, I am bombarding the gates of heaven." He said, "I heard the voice of the Spirit of God speak inside of me: 'Do you know how big heaven is, Kenneth?' 'Yes, it's 1,500 miles square.' The Spirit of God said, 'Considering that My throne is at the center and you are knocking on the gates at the outer edge, you are 750 miles off!' "

What was the problem? Mentally, he was still outside the gate. This was the Jews' problem that the writer of Hebrews addressed. They still had a mentality of an old priesthood. The letter to the Hebrews was written to Jews, while the letter to the Ephesians was written primarily to Gentiles. Paul was saying, "At one time you were a great distance from God, but now you have been brought near by the blood of Jesus Christ." The blood provided the righteousness.

For He Himself is our peace, who has made both one, and has broken down the middle wall of separation.

Ephesians 2:14

18

When you know you are righteous in Christ Jesus, then you will have peace. Paul said, **"For the kingdom of God is not eating and drinking, but righteousness and peace and joy in the Holy Spirit"** (Romans 14:17).

People who try to get joy without being righteous will always end up with shallow, short-lived happiness. When you know you are righteous, you will have peace and joy. Romans 5:1 says, **"Therefore, having been justified by faith, we have peace with God through our Lord Jesus Christ."** No longer is there a war between you and God or a sense of fear.

Isaiah 32:17 says:

> The work of righteousness will be peace, and the effect of righteousness, quietness and assurance forever.

Some people can be in a room by themselves, and while there is an outward quietness, there is a roar going on in their heart because they have no peace in their mind. Other people can be in the middle of a football stadium with 100,000 people in the stands, yet have perfect peace because of what has happened in their life.

If you don't have inner quietness in your heart and mind, it's because of a lack of revelation of righteousness. Many times people try to put band-aids on their problems rather than deal with the root cause. If you will solve the root problem of righteousness, then the fruit of quietness, confidence and assurance will be present. Your understanding of righteousness in Christ is the absolute basis of an effective prayer life.

Gospel Prayer Truths

Here are sixteen gospel prayer truths from Chapter 2:
1. Effective prayer is based upon praying God's Word.
2. The eyes of the Lord are on the righteous, and His ears are open to their prayers (Psalm 34:15; 1 Peter 3:12).

3. Sin will short-circuit an effective prayer life.

4. There is no condemnation to those who are in Christ Jesus who walk according to the Spirit rather than according to the flesh (Romans 8:1).

5. The way you treat people, including family members, will either hinder or enhance your prayer life.

6. The prayers of a righteous person will avail much (James 5: 16).

7. A true intercessor will pray God's will (His Word) into the earth.

8. Knowing that you are the righteousness of God in Christ is the absolute basis of an effective prayer life.

9. Righteousness comes by faith in the complete work of the shed blood of Jesus Christ.

10. To know you are righteous in Christ will deliver you from fear, condemnation, inferiority and guilt.

11. Righteousness comes to those who accept Jesus Christ as their Lord and Savior in exchange for their unrighteousness.

12. When God looks at you in your prayer life, He looks at you through the shed blood of His Son.

13. Anyone who has received God's grace and the gift of righteousness through Jesus Christ will reign in this life (Romans 5:17).

14. When you know who you are in Christ, you will pray with authority.

15. Any believer in Jesus Christ can boldly approach the throne of God's grace to obtain mercy and grace in time of need (Hebrews 4:16).

16. The person who is righteous in Christ will enjoy peace, quietness, confidence and assurance forever (Romans 14:17; Isaiah 32:17).

QUESTIONS

Part 1. Completion

Please complete each of the statements.

1. Prayer is an exchange of divine _____ and
    _____.

2. Success in life depends on your _____ life.

3. Psalm 34:15,16 says, "The eyes of the Lord are on the
    _____, and His ears are open to their cry.
    The face of the Lord is against those who do _____."

4. _____ will block God's blessings from
    reaching you.

5. To set the stage for effectual prayer in your life, you should
    _____ your heart through repentance.

6. There is no _____ to those who
    walk according to the Spirit rather than according to the
    flesh (Romans 8:1).

7. Proper behavior will enhance the _____
    of marriage partners.

8. James said, "The effectual fervent prayer of a righteous
    man _____ much" (James 5:16 KJV).
    The Amplified Translation of this verse says the prayer of
    a righteous person "makes tremendous _____
    available."

9. Elijah, an ordinary human being like you and me, prayed
    that it would not rain. As a result, it did not rain for
    _____ years, until the time he prayed that it would
    rain (James 5:17,18).

10. An intercessor is a person who hears from God and then
    prays His _____ into the earth.

11. Two of the primary reasons Elijah's prayers were so
    effective are:
    a. _____
    b. _____

21

12. The basis of all effective prayer is to know that you are the
    _____ of God in Christ.

13. Righteousness becomes ours when we believe by faith in
    the complete work of the shed _____ of Jesus
    Christ.

14. Righteousness will deliver you from what four negative
    qualities?

    a. _____

    b. _____

    c. _____

    d. _____

15. No one can be righteous by their own efforts. Isaiah 64:6
    says, "All our righteousnesses are like _____
    _____."

16. To understand that you are righteous in Christ Jesus will
    bring Holy Ghost _____ to your prayer life
    and will cause you to pray with _____.

17. Hebrews 4:12 will give you an understanding of why we
    are to pray the Word: "For the word of God is _____
    and _____, and _____ than
    any two-edged sword."

18. Hebrews 4:16 says we can come boldly to the throne of
    grace in prayer and obtain _____ and _____
    to help in time of need.

19. Isaiah 32:17 says the work of righteousness is _____
    and the effect of righteousness is _____
    and _____ forever.

Part 2. Personal Application

Please complete the questions and/or statements to the best of your ability.

1. I need an infusion of divine life in the following area(s):

   _____

   _____

   _____

   _____

   _____

   The Scriptures I am believing for these needs to be met are:

   _____

   _____

   _____

2. I am righteous because _____

   _____

   _____

3. God's ears are open to my prayers because _____

   _____

   _____

   _____

   _____

4. To me, Jesus' act of shedding His blood at Calvary means

   _____

   _____

_____

_____

_____

_____

5. Fear, condemnation, inferiority and guilt have no place in me because _____

_____

_____

_____

_____

_____

CHAPTER 3

Prayer: The Breakfast of Champions

In the realm of the Spirit, the breakfast of champions is early morning prayer. A consistent life of prayer is the basis for a life of continual victories. It is possible for a person to be born again and know Jesus personally, yet fail to have a disciplined, consistent life of prayer, and therefore, fail to experience daily victory.

Jesus ministered to people—the sick and the demon-possessed—late into the night, yet Scripture says He rose up a great while before day and found a quiet place where He could commune with His Father. Jesus knew that His personal victory was dependent upon communion with His Father.

At evening, when the sun had set, they brought to Him all who were sick and those who were demon-possessed.

And the whole city was gathered together at the door.

Then He healed many who were sick with various diseases, and cast out many demons; and He did not allow the demons to speak, because they knew Him.

Now in the morning, having risen a long while before daylight, *He* [Jesus] *went out and departed to a solitary place; and there He prayed.*

Mark 1:32-35

Why Early Morning Prayer?

Here are nine reasons why you should pray at the start of your day.

1. *Jesus did it.* Jesus set the example for us in prayer. He got up early in the morning and found a place where He could be alone to start His day with prayer. Scripture says that Jesus often went into a garden or into the mountains to pray. If Jesus needed to start His day with prayer, how much more do we need to start our days with prayer? He taught us that we could go into our closet alone and pray—wherever your closet or solitary place might be—in an actual closet, under your bed, or in your apartment, house, backyard or neighborhood! The important thing is to find a place where you can communicate with the Lord.

2. *The way you start something has a great effect on the way it ends up.* If you start your day communing with the Lord, very likely you will be in communion with Him throughout your day.

Think about it. If you are going to paint a house white and you start out with green paint, you are going to be in trouble! Big trouble! The way you start out can have a definite effect on the way it will look in the end!

In our church, we have a great time of worship, testimonies, sharing, singing and hearing the Word, but you cannot live on one spiritual meal a week. Your physical strength is in direct proportion to the energy that you take in through the food that you eat. It's the same way with communion with God. We need more than one spiritual meal a week to be strong in the Lord and in the power of His might.

In Oklahoma, when you travel on one of our turnpikes, if you don't start out the right direction, you could be in trouble. If you are going to Oklahoma City from Tulsa and someone says, "Go on I-44," and you get on I-44 going northeast, you could end up in Joplin, Missouri, instead of Oklahoma City. You might make good time, the car might run smoothly and you might enjoy the scenery, but you will end up in the wrong place if you start out wrong.

There are places along the turnpike where you can get off and make a turnaround. You may lose some time, but you can make some changes. Even though people may have some bad starts, the good news is, there is redemption and we can turn around and go the right direction. Each day is a new day. Why not start out right instead of having to turn around in the middle of the day?

Let's assume you are taking Flight 34A to New York City. You forget whether it is "A" or "B," and you get on "B" and end up in Los Angeles. There is no turning around at 35,000 feet in the air! Sometimes people are unable to turn around because of circumstances and situations.

When a sailboat starts out, the way the sails are set determines the direction the boat will go. The way you set your sails at the start of your day determines the course you will follow during the day. The good news is, if you set your sails to catch the wind in the right way, you will head on the right course, and there is a good possibility if you keep adjusting the sails during the day, you will reach the right destination. If you start each day right with God, you can enjoy the trip and wind up at the right place.

3. *When you pray early in your day, you will get an attitude adjustment!*

It has also been said that attitude determines altitude. How high you go in life will be determined by your attitude. The pitch of an airplane determines how high it will fly. If the nose is turned upward, it can fly higher if there is appropriate power.

Our lives are the same way. If we haven't set our lives in the right direction, we will continue to fly on a straight course and never gain any altitude. But when we start our day by setting our affection on God, something happens and we begin to climb higher and higher. If our attitude is set on things above, we will

27

go with God. But if we never set our sails, our sights, or our plans any higher than going through the motions, just making a living, or going through the routine, then life goes on at a snail's pace drudgery. Even though the scenery may be good, you will get to a place and ask, "Why am I here?"

I believe many Christians are in crisis in their lives right now because they know what is right, they know the Word and they have heard the truth, but there is no practical daily application of it by starting their day in prayer.

4. *It is important to start your day with prayer because many interruptions come in the middle of the day.*

Pray through your schedule each day. Pray through each thing that you know is going to happen. Ask the Lord for direction, and ask Him to prioritize your activities.

Many people jump out of bed, run for breakfast, go to work and sometime in the middle of the day, they might think about God. But they might not, because the schedule is so demanding, there are so many people wanting their time and so many things that have to be done.

It's possible to go all through your day and not think about God until you pop your Bible open and have a word of prayer right before going to bed. I believe the crises people face can be solved if they will meet Jesus first thing in the morning.

5. *When you are hungry for fellowship with God, you will take time for early morning prayer.*

First John 1:3 says, **"Our fellowship is with the Father and with His Son Jesus Christ."**

Because some people work a night shift, I understand that their day may not start early in the morning. The key, however, is to set a time, preferably at the start of your day, to fellowship with the Father, Son and Holy Spirit. Second Corinthians 13:14 says we have communion with the Holy Spirit as well as with the Father and Son.

Scripture also says God never leaves, forsakes, or abandons us.
I will not in any way fail you nor give you up nor leave you without support. [I will] not, [I will] not, [I will] not in any degree leave you helpless nor forsake nor let [you] down (relax My hold on you)! [Assuredly not!]

Hebrews 13:5 AMP

The Lord is with me all through my day. I don't just meet Him in the morning and leave Him in the prayer closet. He is with me, whether I pray or whether I don't pray, whether I think about Him or whether I don't think about Him. But something happens when I take the time to listen to what He has to say and talk to Him before I start my day.

The summer I was nineteen I worked at the Boys' Club, my wife-to-be, Sharon, and her family moved out of town. I worked 12-hour days, so a friend at the Club and I played ping pong once or twice a week late in the afternoon during a break. We could tell who had seen their girlfriend most recently, because that person always won!

Sharon is wonderful and families are wonderful, but there is just something about having a quiet time alone with the Lord. If you spend time with Him, you will be on top.

Imagine a man saying to his wife, "Honey, you are in my thoughts all day long, but I just haven't got time to talk to you. I've got a picture of you, and I am going to remember you, but I don't have time to talk to you." The next day she says, "I'd like to spend a little time alone with you so we can go over something." You respond, "I don't have time to be with you, but I will remember you." You go through that routine for a few months, and your relationship will grow cold, because relationships are built on an interchange that is alive, continuous and flowing.

That's the way some people are with their Christian experience. They say, "God, You are in my thoughts. You are always

29

with me," but they never spend time alone with Him in prayer.

Thank God you can pray over your typewriter, computer, sales desk or whatever it is. But there needs to be a time when you put all these things aside and place all of your focus on Him where God has an opportunity to talk to you without distractions and you have an opportunity to talk to Him.

Some people say, "I'm bored with Christianity." It's because they are running through the motions of living but they don't have a relationship. I have faced it with many people. Some are churchgoers, but they don't know Jesus. There is no intimate fellowship with Him. There is no desire to be with Him.

You need a relationship with Jesus every day. Just having your name on a church roll isn't salvation. Just showing up in a building doesn't give you a relationship with Christ. But when you start your day by magnifying and praising the Lord, you will develop a relationship with Him.

6. *Just as you would fill your gas tank before you start out on a trip, you need to fill your mind with God's Word and prayer before you start your day.* Then you are prepared for the reversals, emotional situations and bad attitudes that you may encounter during the day.

One of the reasons for a lack of control over appetite, anger and wrong thoughts could be because those things aren't set in order at the start of the day. All the frustrations and hassles we face could be because we haven't won the battle in prayer before we started the day. Problems arise and demands come up, and sometimes there is more demand than there is of you! You can only go so long with your exports exceeding your imports. If you don't fuel up on the Word and prayer before you start your day, you could reach a trade deficit! Some Christians are in that deficit. They know Christ, but there is more demanded of them than is being put back into their lives.

You can deplete a soil by continually growing the same crop

on it year after year. I remember talking with a farmer who planted beans one year and then planted wheat on the same ground the following year for the replenishing of the soil. Just as the soil must be properly nourished, you need to build yourself back up. Too many people are running on empty.

Though God may be in your thoughts all the time and dwell on the inside of you through the Holy Spirit, there is just something about setting aside time to be alone with Him.

7. *In Exodus 16, the Lord told the children of Israel to get their manna before the sun got hot on the ground.* Manna is Living Bread—Jesus Christ. That means to get a fresh word from heaven from the Word of God before you start your day. There's just something about getting up early to gather your manna at the start of the day.

People who don't set their sails on God early in the day many times forget about Him during the day, and they go in the power of their own flesh.

When I was first born again, I went to work at 7:00 a.m. in the oil fields. I don't know how the importance of early morning prayer got into me, but I got up early and went out on my back porch to pray before I went to work. With the bunch that I was working with, I needed prayer! It was one of the roughest groups of people I have ever been around. Their language was bad, and their attitude toward me wasn't great either, because I was the youngest and I was a Christian.

Maybe you work around situations where you are picked on or you hear negative or unclean things. Prayer builds an insulation in our lives so we aren't demoralized, depressed, or intimidated by what happens around us.

All through my years, I can remember the places of prayer where I took time to be alone with the Lord before getting into the activities of my day. The power of early morning prayer will be evidenced in our lives.

31

Years ago, I talked with a contractor who got up at 5:00 a.m. to seek God in prayer. He had many people reporting to him and he dealt with several subcontractors throughout the day. He said, "There is no way I can make it through my day unless I meet God and spend time with Him the first part of the day."

The report I heard about this man even before I met him was, "He commits every morning to God in prayer, and God has used his business to be a witness to the entire community."

When you, as a business person, will seek God the first thing in the morning, then God will permeate your work and your business with His presence. If God's presence permeates your life, it will go right through into your workers and into your business, and there will be honesty, integrity, faithfulness, loyalty and commitment.

Sometimes people tend to think that they are too busy to have early morning prayer. I believe it's just the opposite. The more demanding your schedule, the greater the need for early morning prayer.

One great preacher said that because the morning is the gate of the entire day, it should be well guarded with prayer. Starting your day with prayer anchors your whole day in God.

You don't have to look very far, even in Christian circles, to see that it looks like some people have all their moorings cut, their anchors severed and they are simply drifting on the sea of life with no purpose. They are unable to handle the daily challenges that come.

As a single parent, you need to be in prayer every day for God's wisdom in training your children. As a single person, you need to be in prayer every day to overcome the temptations you face. If you are married, you need to be in prayer every day to keep your marriage strong. Whatever your age or vocation, prayer is vital to success.

When the gate of your day is guarded with prayer, the devil

won't be able to gain entrance into your life because you will be alert to his tactics. Without early morning prayer, however, people's minds and spirits aren't alert to the voice of God. But when you get up in the morning and God speaks to you at the start of your day, it will carry you, guard you and keep you on course with the Spirit of God.

To start your day without prayer is comparable to starting your day without washing and dressing. You wouldn't dare go to the job, the office, the business, or the plant without preparing yourself physically. Yet, how many people put more emphasis on the outer man than they do on the inner man? They are all dressed up on the outside, but on the inside, their soul is not guarded against the devil's attacks.

With what is happening in the world right now, unless we have our lives anchored in prayer on a daily basis, we will not be able to stand. Too many people have already been blown completely out of the water. They are shipwrecked in their faith because they have neglected prayer. They have neglected to spend time alone with God in His Word, in hearing from Him and in fellowshipping with Him.

If you don't start your day with God, the devil will come before you ever get out of bed and bombard you with negative, defeating thoughts. Before you get out of bed, you will have a schedule that ten people couldn't accomplish, and it is a weight on you all day long, trying to get through things that God didn't design or direct. But when you wait on the Lord early in the morning, God will clarify your priorities.

Too many people major on the minors and minor on the majors, spending their lives in things that are fruitless because they never got God's priorities. Managing our lives is one of the greatest needs we have in this hour.

A morning time of prayer and fellowship with the Father, Son and Holy Spirit has meant everything in the world to me. My ministry would be weak, powerless and ineffective without it.

Is your Christian life powerful and full of the fruit of the Spirit? Is there success and blessing in your life that's spilling out onto the lives of other people? Or is it merely a treadmill that's going faster and faster and the incline is getting steeper and steeper and there seems to be no end?

To give God the first part of your day in prayer is part of the price of spiritual power and prosperity. It costs you nothing but an earnest desire for God's best. Why not give the best part of your day to God? If you give God your best and commit it totally to Him, you can expect God's best to come back to you.

8. *When you start your time of prayer with praise to the Lord, you will receive revelation, instruction, inspiration, strength, peace, deliverance from temptation, refreshing and restoration.*

Psalm 63:1 says, **"O God, You are my God; early will I seek You...."**

Psalm 100:4 says, **"Enter into His gates with thanksgiving, and into His courts with praise. Be thankful to Him, and bless His name."**

The prophet Isaiah, by the inspiration of the Holy Spirit, said:

> **Have you not known? Have you not heard? The everlasting God, the Lord, the Creator of the ends of the earth, neither faints nor is weary. His understanding is unsearchable.**
>
> **He gives power to the weak, and to those who have no might He increases strength.**
>
> **Even the youths shall faint and be weary, and the young men shall utterly fall,**
>
> **But those who wait on the Lord shall renew their strength; they shall mount up with wings like eagles, they shall run and not be weary, they shall walk and not faint.**
>
> **Isaiah 40:28-31**

People faint and become weary when they do not wait upon the Lord in a time dedicated to prayer.

When people talk about how weary they are and how difficult their spiritual life is, they are giving evidence that their prayer life has ebbed away, because Scripture says that those who wait upon the Lord will renew their strength. They will exchange their weakness for God's strength. They will mount up with wings as eagles. Thank God that we can move from being turkeys to becoming eagles!

9. *Giving God the first part of your day is a spiritual law of giving the firstfruits.* If you give God the first part of your day, He will multiply time back to you.

Proverbs 3:5,6 says:

Trust in the Lord with all your heart, and lean not on your own understanding;
In all your ways acknowledge Him, and He shall direct your paths.

God will guide the path you take if you pray over it. But if you don't acknowledge God and ask for His wisdom, He could be standing right in front of you with the answers to every problem you are facing, but you are too busy trying to solve your own problems and trying to make things happen in the flesh.

Scripture says, **"God resists the proud..."** (James 4:6). When you think you can handle your day without God, that is *pride.* God will resist you, and you won't have His blessings and His answers. Whatever you can do in your own ability is what will be done. But if you will say, "Lord, I humble myself, I need Your help today," He will give you grace.

James 4:8 says, **"Draw near to God and He will draw near to you...."**

There is a teaching among secular corporate leaders that their most productive time is at the start of the day. They are encouraged to take time to be quiet and listen before they start their obligations.

The natural human spirit, when it is tranquil, will think of things that need to be done and will set things in order. How much more productive we will be with the anointing of the Holy Spirit, the power of the Word of God, a tranquil human spirit and a mind that says, "Lord, I want Your divine direction today."

Is there a glow on your face and victory in your step when you hit your work? Or is there a growl? If someone speaks to you, is it like hitting the neighbor's dog with a stick or biting their head off?

God wants to speak to you in early morning prayer. If you take time to listen, you will hear God speak. Many people have said, "I haven't heard from God." I ask, "Have you listened? Have you given God an opportunity to speak to you?"

As you read your Bible and pray for God's will to be done, confess God's promises and listen, write down the things God is speaking to you. In this way, you will begin to manage your life every day. No one cares more about you than Jesus Christ, and if you will let Him direct your steps, the pathway He leads you on will cause you to prosper.

Gospel Prayer Truths

Here are fifteen gospel prayer truths from Chapter 3:

1. In the realm of the Spirit, early morning prayer is the breakfast of champions!

2. Jesus set an example for us to start each day with prayer (Mark 1:35).

3. The way you set your sails at the start of your day will determine the course you follow during the day.

4. How high the altitude you achieve in life is determined by your attitude.

5. Relationships are built on an interchange that is alive, continuous and flowing.

6. You can win over the day's challenges and obstacles in prayer *before* you start your day.

7. Prayer builds an insulation in our lives so we aren't demoralized, depressed, or intimidated by what happens around us.

8. The more demanding your schedule, the greater the need for early morning prayer.

9. When the gate of your day is guarded with prayer, the devil won't be able to gain entrance into your life because you will be alert to his tactics.

10. You will never be shipwrecked in your faith if you spend time in early morning prayer and in the Word.

11. God will clarify your day's priorities in your time of early morning prayer.

12. To give God the first part of your day in prayer is part of the price of spiritual power and authority.

13. To wait upon the Lord in a time of prayer will cause your strength to be renewed (Isaiah 40:31).

14. As you acknowledge the Lord, He will direct your paths (Proverbs 3:6).

15. As you draw near to God, He will draw near to you (James 4:8).

QUESTIONS

Part 1. Completion

Please complete each of the statements.

1. A consistent _____ life is the basis for a life of continual victories.

2. Jesus is our example in prayer. He knew that personal victory was dependent upon daily _____ with His Father.

3. Early morning prayer will give you an _____ adjustment.

4. Your attitude will determine your _____ in life.

5. Just as you would fill your gas tank before starting out on a trip, before you start your day you should fill your mind with:

   a. _____

   b. _____

6. You should spend time alone to gather Living Bread—a time alone with _____ _____—before you start your day.

7. When you wait on the Lord early in the morning, He will clarify your _____ for the day.

8. To give God the first part of your day in prayer is part of the price of spiritual _____ and _____.

9. According to Pastor Daugherty, when you start your time of prayer with praise, you will receive what eight things?

   a. _____

   b. _____

   c. _____

d. _____

e. _____

f._____

g. _____

h. _____

10. According to the prophet Isaiah, when you wait upon the Lord, four things will happen. Please name them (Isaiah 40:31):

a. _____

b. _____

c._____

d. _____

11. According to Proverbs 3:6, as you acknowledge the Lord in all of your ways, He will _____ your paths.

Part 2. Personal Application

Please complete the questions and/or statements to the best of your ability.

1. Early morning prayer—the breakfast of champions—to me means_____
_____
_____
_____
_____

2. My favorite quiet place for time alone with Jesus is
_____
_____

_____
_____
_____

3. The way I "set my sails" for each day is_____
_____
_____
_____
_____

4. The way I wait upon the Lord is to_____
_____
_____
_____
_____

The result is_____
_____
_____
_____
_____

CHAPTER 4

A PATTERN FOR PRAYER

Many people have never had a pattern or an example to follow in prayer. I learned a lot about prayer from Sharon's father.

Jesus gave us guidelines for a life of prayer, which, if followed, will undergird us in the fulfillment of God's destiny for our lives. He is our example in prayer.

> **And when you pray, you shall not be like the hypocrites. For they love to pray standing in the synagogues and on the corners of the streets, that they may be seen by men. Assuredly, I say to you, they have their reward.**
>
> **Matthew 6:5**

The word *hypocrite* has to do with an actor, a farce, something that isn't real, genuine, or sincere. Jesus was saying, "The hypocrites pray for the acclaim of men."

You can go in the ditch on either side. You can pray to be seen of men, or you can get to the point where you are paranoid and afraid that someone will see you praying. Jesus prayed with His disciples.

I have had people ask me, "Why do we pray corporately in the church?" We're not praying to be seen of men, but the primary motivation for corporate prayer is that one can put a thousand to flight, while two can put ten thousand to flight (Deuteronomy 32:30).

In Acts 4, after Peter and John were taken into custody and

later released for preaching in Jesus' name, they returned to their own company where they **"raised their voice to God with one accord..."** (Acts 4:24). They prayed aloud as a group.

There is nothing wrong with public prayer out loud, but Jesus basically said, "Don't be like the hypocrites who pray just to be seen of men." They wanted others to see them praying so they would be considered "spiritual."

Jesus continued:

> **But you, when you pray, go into your room, and when you have shut your door, pray to your Father who is in the secret place; and your Father who sees in secret will reward you openly.**

> **Matthew 6:6**

Jesus wasn't saying that the only place to pray is in your closet. The idea He was trying to convey was to find a place alone for private prayer.

> **And when you pray, do not use vain repetitions as the heathen do. For they think that they will be heard for their many words.**

> **Matthew 6:7**

Maybe you learned to pray a set pattern of words and a repetition of praises. God is not impressed with vain repetitions, which is an "empty" recital of words!

John 4:23,24 says:

> **But the hour is coming, and now is, when the true worshippers will worship the Father in spirit and truth; for the Father is seeking such to wor ship Him.**

> **God is Spirit, and those who worship Him must worship in spirit and truth.**

I interpret this to mean that we are to pray in genuine, heartfelt sincerity out of our spirit rather than recital from memory. Jesus was saying, "Vain repetition won't get God's ear."

Therefore do not be like them. For your Father knows the things you have need of before you ask Him.

Matthew 6:8

If God knows everything we need before we ask, why should we ask? Why doesn't He just fix our problems? We are His children, we are in relationship with Him, yet we are told to ask.

When God made man in the beginning, He gave him dominion over the earth and placed him in a position of legal authority in the earth. When Adam and Eve sinned, that authority was transferred into the hands of the devil. Illegally, immorally and unethically by deceit, Satan became the god of this world's system. Jesus called him the prince of the power of the air in this world. Satan took authority by the default of Adam and Eve through sin.

At Calvary, Jesus regained that authority, for He said in Matthew 28:18, **"All authority has been given to Me in heaven and on earth."** As believers, we have been given the right and authority to call those things forth into the earth that are God's will for us.

Let's assume you are in a position of authority for the security of a building. If you don't see that the building is secured, even though you have the keys, the doors won't be locked. You have to lock them.

It's the same way in prayer. God has given us the keys—the ability—to bind and loose, but we have to do it (Matthew 18:18).

We are the enforcers of the will of God in the earth. In other words, God has a plan, but it can only be enforced when we speak it forth. This is why we continually refer to the power of confession—the law of speaking God's Word and agreeing with God in prayer. It is crucial to say what God says, because God performs His Word (Jeremiah 1:12).

John Wesley, founder of Methodism, said, "It seems that God will do nothing except someone prays." The idea that is propagated in some circles is that God is sovereign so He can do anything He wants to do. In other words, "He can change His mind on a daily basis. He can alter His course. You never know what God is going to do, because He is sovereign." That is an extreme teaching, and out of it comes, "It may not be God's will to heal you because He is sovereign." Regarding accidents and calamities, some people say, "God is sovereign. He chose to do that." Satan will rip you off in health and finances, and he will dominate your life and the lives of your children with this kind of thinking.

When you align this kind of thinking with the Word, you will see that it is inaccurate because God's Word says, **"I am the Lord, I do not change..."** (Malachi 3:6). **"Jesus Christ is the same yesterday, today, and forever"** (Hebrews 13:8).

God is constant. He does not change. He is love. He is a God of faith. His mercy endures forever, and it is new every morning.

Another inaccurate extreme of the sovereignty of God is, "If God has willed for people to be saved, they will be saved whether you do anything about it or not. Therefore, there's no need to witness, because God is going to save certain people."

God is a sovereign God, but He has sovereignly chosen to work in certain ways in the earth. One of the primary ways He works is in response to believing prayer.

He said:

> **If My people who are called by My name will humble themselves, and pray and seek My face, and turn from their wicked ways, then I will hear from heaven, and will forgive their sin and heal their land.**

> **2 Chronicles 7:14**

People who are into the sovereignty teaching say, "You can't just say God is going to do this, because you are putting Him in a box." I say, "If you can't, how do you know you are saved?"

The Bible says, **"For whoever calls upon the name of the Lord shall be saved"** (Romans 10:13). That's not putting God in, a box. That is obeying the Word of God and getting in His box!

Some people say, "To confess and declare things is like bossing God around." No! God is bossing us around! He is the boss. He is Lord. He is the One Who said to speak in alignment with His Word.

Prayer is basically taking God at His Word. It is believing and speaking in agreement with what God says. I believe that I receive when I pray.

Jesus said in Mark 11:24:

> **Therefore I say to you, whatever things you ask when you pray, believe that you receive them, and you will have them.**

When I pray in alignment with God's Word, I release my faith by saying, "Thank You, Lord, for meeting this need, for making this provision, for opening this door."

Our prayers are to be directed to the Father in Jesus' name.

> **And whatever you ask in My name, that I will do, that the Father may be glorified in the Son.**
> **If you ask anything in My name, I will do it.**
>
> **John 14:13,14**

The "ACTS" Prayer Pattern

There are several "patterns" of prayer. Sometimes I pray the "ACTS" pattern, which originated with the Navigators:

A	=	Adoration
C	=	Confession
T	=	Thanksgiving
S	=	Supplication

The Lord's Prayer

Another pattern of prayer is using the "Lord's Prayer" as a model. Jesus offered this pattern of prayer for the disciples:

Hallowed Be Your Name...

In this manner, therefore, pray: Our Father in heaven, hallowed be Your name.

Matthew 6:9

The Lord's Prayer is a "model prayer" rather than a repetitious prayer.

Hallowed means "exalted, honored, or reverenced." The Lord's Prayer begins with worship. Divine protocol for entering the presence of the Father is to start your prayer with praise and worship. In the natural, when you go into a statehouse or a governmental setting, there is a protocol of how to address the king, the president, or the leader.

One of the things we have learned through the years is that God reveals Himself by many names, so as you worship and honor Him, you are honoring Him as:

Jehovah-Jireh – Your Provider, Source and Sufficiency.

Jehovah Rapha (or Rophe) – Your Healer, Health and Physician.

Jehovah-Nissi – Your banner of Victory.

Jehovah-M'Kaddesh – Your Sanctifier, Light and Holiness.

Jehovah-Rohi – Your Shepherd, Protector and Guide.

Jehovah-Shalom – Your Peace, Comfort and Security.

Jehovah-Shammah – Your omnipresent (ever-present) Friend.

Jehovah-Tsidkenu – Your Righteousness.

These are Old Testament names through which God revealed His very nature. He was also called Elohim, the Lord exalted and most high, and El Shaddai, the God Who is more than enough.

Sometimes I spend thirty minutes in worship of Jehovah-Jireh alone. Instead of coming to the Father in prayer, saying, "My name is Jimmy, gimme, gimme, gimme," you can worship Him through His names which reveal Who He really is.

Your Will Be Done...

> **Your kingdom come. Your will be done on earth
> as it is in heaven.**
>
> **Matthew 6:10**

You can declare your allegiance to the King of kings and with your own mouth order your life by the rule of His Kingdom. You can declare, "Lord, Your will be done in earth as it is in heaven."

As a believer, you have been given authority and power, but it is up to you to use it and release it. God will perform His Word, and He will move in response to what you say, because authority is released through words. Declare that His Kingdom has come in your life.

The will of God is that you would be saved and filled with the Holy Spirit. The will of God is that you would be sanctified and separated unto Him

> **Now may the God of peace Himself sanctify you
> completely; and may your whole spirit, soul, and
> body be preserved blameless at the coming of our
> Lord Jesus Christ.**
>
> **1 Thessalonians 5:23**

God's will is that **"all men...be saved and...come to the knowledge of the truth"** (1 Timothy 2:4). God's will is that **"you may prosper in all things and be in health, just as your soul prospers"** (3 John 2). God's will is that governments would exalt Him. "Lord, let Your Kingdom come in every area of our lives."

I pray over my spirit, soul and body. When I pray over my spirit, I pray Galatians 5:22,23 because the fruit of the Spirit is love, joy, peace, longsuffering, kindness, goodness, faithfulness, gentleness and self-control.

Pray Philippians 4:8 KJV over your mind:

> **Finally, brethren, whatsoever things are true,
> whatsoever things are honest, whatsoever things are**

47

just, whatsoever things are pure, whatsoever things
are lovely, whatsoever things are of good report; if
there be any virtue, and if there be any praise, think
on these things.

Then pray over your body according to 1 Corinthians 6:19 20:

Or do you not know that your body is the
temple of the Holy Spirit who is in you, whom you
have from God, and you are not your own?

For you were bought at a price; therefore glorify
God in your body and in your spirit, which are
God's.

As an example of how to pray over your mind and body, you
can say: "Lord, Your will be done in my body. Lungs, heart,
blood, immune system, cells, every part of my body, the will of
God be done in you. Lord, I pray today that everything I think
and do, and what I hear, see and act upon, would be according to
Your will."

Then pray over your own family. I pray, "Lord, Your will be
done in Sarah, Ruth, John and Paul and in my wife, Sharon. Your
Kingdom come and Your will be done." I include my mother,
brothers and Sharon's family—praying for the Kingdom of God
to come in each of us.

I pray for the will of God to be done in our church. I pray for
our outreaches into the nursing homes, government-subsidized
housing projects, the bus ministry, nursery, children, youth,
singles, Sunday school, the Bible Institute, the Christian school,
the missions training center and all points in between, "Lord, Your
will be done." As you are praying this way, you can focus on an
area as the Holy Spirit leads you.

Lastly, I pray for our government. In writing to Timothy, Paul
said:

Therefore I exhort first of all that supplications,
prayers, intercessions, and giving of thanks be made
for all men,

For kings and all who are in authority, that we may lead a quiet and peaceable life in all godliness and reverence.

For this is good and acceptable in the sight of God our Savior.

1 Timothy 2:1-3

Why should we pray for government leaders? Where there is peace and quiet, the gospel can flow freely. In a war-torn country, it is very difficult for the gospel to flow forth. After the war is over, people are more open and receptive, but generally, war does not produce an atmosphere for preaching. People pray in foxholes, but the Bible says to pray that we may lead a quiet and peaceable life.

Scripture says, **"You will hear of wars and rumors of wars..."** (Matthew 24:6), but it also says, **"Pray for the peace of Jerusalem..."** (Psalm 122:6). We are to pray for peace in our lives and in our nations, so start by praying for the will of God to be done in your own government, starting at the top. "Lord, I pray that Your will be done in the president, the vice-president, the cabinet, the chiefs of staff, the Congress, the Supreme Court justices, the governors, state representatives, mayors and city councilmen."

Give Us This Day Our Daily Bread...

Once you have prayed over yourself, your family, your church and your government, you are ready to pray Matthew 6:11, **"Give us this day our daily bread."** There are two aspects to this verse: 1) Revelation knowledge or spiritual bread; and 2) Natural food.

Jesus said, **"I am the bread of life. He who comes to Me shall never hunger, and he who believes in Me shall never thirst"** (John 6:35). In Matthew 4:4, Jesus said, **"Man shall not live by bread alone, but by every word that proceeds from the mouth of God."**

The bread of heaven is the revelation knowledge of Jesus Christ, which is what we are to live by. You can pray, "Lord, give me this day the portion of Your Word that I need." You can gather fresh manna from heaven every day. Six days a week the Israelites gathered fresh manna, and they had to gather it before the sun reflected on the ground. This is why we are to participate in early morning prayer. Before the sun gets hot on the ground, we can pray and receive fresh manna from heaven.

The second aspect of praying for daily bread is the natural food that we need. Sometimes we need bread to spend, so we should pray, "Lord, give me some dough!" This refers to the present-day things that we need. Obviously, Jesus is revealing the will of the Father, and we are to pray, "Lord, give us this day our daily bread."

Forgive Us As We Forgive Others...

> **And forgive us our debts, as we forgive our debtors.**
>
> **Matthew 6:12**

Prayer is to incorporate forgiveness, mercy and grace. "Lord, help me to be merciful. I forgive and release those who have hurt or offended me. I won't hold an offense." Then ask forgiveness for the things you have done or said that were wrong and for the things you failed to do. Forgiveness of yourself and others is coupled together. Jesus further explained the principle of forgiveness in verses 14 and 15:

> **For if you forgive men [others] their trespasses, your heavenly Father will also forgive you.**
> **But if you do not forgive men their trespasses, neither will your Father forgive your trespasses.**

Unforgiveness, bitterness and resentment are common characteristics of people who have psychological problems. Happy people are forgivers. Miserable, depressed people are not. Regardless of what has happened to you, if you will forgive, you can have the joy of the Lord in your life. No man can take that joy away from you unless you choose to be unforgiving. If you forgive, you will live in the blessings of God. If you are merciful, you will obtain mercy. The Kingdom of God is built on the principles of love, mercy and forgiveness.

Lead Us Not Into Temptation...

> **And do not lead us into temptation, but deliver us from the evil one....**
>
> **Matthew 6:13**

James says:

> **Let no one say when he is tempted, "I am tempted by God"; for God cannot be tempted by evil, nor does He Himself tempt anyone.**
>
> **But each one is tempted when he is drawn away by his own desires and enticed.**
>
> **Then, when desire has conceived, it gives birth to sin; and sin, when it is full-grown, brings forth death.**
>
> **James 1:13-15**

James was saying, "Pray that you would not be led into temptation, but that you would be delivered from all kinds of evil." That includes physical, mental, emotional, spiritual, sexual and financial.

Jesus described the devil's characteristics in John 10:10: stealing, killing and destroying. As a child of God, Jesus has given you the authority to exercise your faith to be delivered from all kinds of evil.

Exalt the Lord!

Jesus ends the Lord's Prayer with a confession of exaltation to the Father. **"For Yours is the kingdom and the power and the glory forever. Amen"** (Matthew 6:13). The devil doesn't have the kingdom, the power and the glory. It belongs to God.

Everything that God is, *He is to you.* **"It is your Father's good pleasure to give you the kingdom"** (Luke 12:32).

You can pray, "Lord, thank You for letting me into Your Kingdom. Thank You for letting Your glory come into my life. It is Your will that I have the spirit of power, love and a sound mind. I am grateful, Lord Jesus, that You brought me into the Kingdom for such a time as this!"

Gospel Prayer Truths

Here are twenty-three gospel prayer truths from Chapter 4:

1. A life of prayer will undergird you in the fulfillment of God's destiny for your life.

2. The primary purpose for corporate prayer is that one can put a thousand to flight, while two can put ten thousand to flight (Deuteronomy 32:30).

3. Vain repetition won't get God's ear, but communication from genuine, heartfelt sincerity will.

4. As believers in Jesus Christ, we have been given the same authority He had in the earth (Matthew 28:18). It is up to us to exercise this authority.

5. God has given us the ability to bind and loose in prayer, but we have to do it (Matthew 18:18).

6. Believers are the enforcers of God's will in the earth.

7. In prayer, we must speak what God says, because He will perform His Word (Jeremiah 1:12).

8. One of the primary ways God works in the earth is in response to believing prayer.

9. God will heal your land—your marriage and family and other relationships, your emotions, finances, or whatever

needs to be healed—when you humble yourself, pray, seek His face and turn from your wicked ways (2 Chronicles 7:14).

10. Prayer is believing and speaking in agreement with what God says.

11. Prayer is to be directed to the Father in Jesus' name.

12. Divine protocol for entering God's presence in prayer is to worship and praise Him.

13. To honor God as Jehovah-Jireh is to honor Him as your Provider, Source and Sufficiency.

14. To honor God as Jehovah-Rapha (or Rophe) is to honor Him as your Healer, health and Physician.

15. To honor God as Jehovah-Nissi is to honor Him as your banner of victory.

16. To honor God as Jehovah-M'Kaddesh is to honor Him as your Sanctifier, Light and Holiness.

17. To honor God as Jehovah-Rohi is to honor Him as your Shepherd, Protector and Guide.

18. To honor God as Jehovah-Shalom is to honor Him as your Peace, Comfort and Security.

19. To honor God as Jehovah-Shammah is to honor Him as your ever-present Friend.

20. To honor God as Jehovah-Tsidkenu is to honor Him as your Righteousness.

21. Authority is released through your words.

22. You are to pray for kings, presidents, government leaders and everyone in positions of authority that you may lead a quiet and peaceable life (1 Timothy 2:2).

23. Prayer is to incorporate forgiveness, mercy and grace.

QUESTIONS

Part 1. Completion

Please complete each of the statements.

1. The primary motivation for corporate prayer is that one can put a _____ to flight, but two can put _____ _____ to flight (Deuteronomy 32:30).

2. True worshippers are those who worship the Father in _____ and _____. (John 4:23,24).

3. Satan became the god of this world's system when Adam and Eve sinned. However, at Calvary, Jesus regained the authority which Adam and Eve lost, and it has been given to every believer. Using this authority, we are to _____ those things forth into the earth that are God's will.

4. God has given us the keys (or ability) to _____ and _____ in prayer (Matthew 18:18).

5. According to 2 Chronicles 7:14, if believers in Jesus Christ will humble themselves and pray, seek God's face and turn from their wicked ways, God will do what three things?

   a. _____

   b. _____

   c. _____

6. Prayer is basically taking God at _____ _____

7. Jesus said, "Therefore I say to you, whatever things you ask when you pray, _____ that you _____ them, and you will have them" (Mark 11:24).

8. Proper protocol in prayer is to approach the Father in _____ name.

9. Jesus said, "If you ask anything in _____ _____, I will do it" (John 14:14).

10. The Navigators' pattern of prayer is:

    A = _____

    C = _____

    T = _____

    S = _____

11. "The Lord's Prayer" found in Matthew 6 is a _____
    prayer rather than a repetitious prayer.

12. Divine protocol for entering the presence of the Lord is
    _____ and _____.

13. Please give a brief description of each of the Old Testament
    names for God through which His nature is revealed:
    a.   Jehovah-Jireh – _____
    b.   Jehovah-Rapha (or Rophe) – _____
         _____
    c.   Jehovah-Nissi – _____
    d.   Jehovah-M'Kaddesh – _____
         _____
    e.   Jehovah-Rohi – _____
    f.   Jehovah-Shalom – _____
    g.   Jehovah-Shammah – _____
         _____
    h.   Jehovah-Tsidkenu – _____

14. One of the names of God, "El Shaddai," means "The God
    Who is _____ than enough."

15. First Timothy 2:4 says that it is God's will for _____
    men to be saved and come to a knowledge of the truth.

16. God's will for all believers is that we _____
    and be in _____, just as our soul prospers with
    the Word (3 John 2).

17. The Spirit of God through Paul gave us eight types of things we are to think on in Philippians 4:8. Please name them:

   a. _____

   b. _____

   c. _____

   d. _____

   e. _____

   f. _____

   g. _____

   h. _____

18. Paul says in 1 Corinthians 6:19,20 that our bodies are the temple of the _____ _____, and we are to _____ God in our body and in our spirit.

19. According to Paul, the result of praying for all men, for kings and for all who are in authority is so we may lead _____ and _____ lives in all godliness and reverence (1 Timothy 2:1,2).

20. To pray for daily bread means to pray for both _____ and _____ food.

21. Jesus said, "I am the _____ of life. He who comes to Me shall never _____ and he who believes in Me shall never _____ " (John 6:35).

22. The bread of heaven refers to the _____ knowledge of Jesus Christ.

23. You can gather fresh manna from heaven every day by studying _____ _____ and meditating upon it.

24. Prayer incorporates _____, _____ and _____.

25. Three common characteristics of people who have psychological problems are:

    a. _____

    b. _____

    c. _____

26. The Kingdom of God is built on the principles of _____

    _____ and _____.

27. James says God cannot be tempted by evil, nor does He tempt anyone with evil. A person is tempted and enticed because of his own fleshly _____ (James 1:14).

28. When desire is conceived, it gives birth to _____ and _____, when it is full-grown, brings forth death (James 1:15).

29. Satan's three primary characteristics, as described in John 10:10, are:

    a. _____

    b. _____

    c. _____

30. In Luke 12:32, Jesus said, "It is your Father's good pleasure to give you the _____."

Part 2. Personal Application

Please complete the questions and/or statements to the best of your ability.

1. As a born-again believer, I have been given authority through Jesus Christ to _____

_____

_____

2. According to 2 Chronicles 7:14, if I will humble myself, pray seek God's face and turn from wickedness, He will heal my land. To me, this means_____

_____

_____

_____

_____

3. Of the eight Old Testament names for God, the nature of God I have experienced most is

_____

_____

_____

_____

_____

_____

4. To think God's thoughts, I_____

_____

_____

_____

_____

_____

5. To bring my body into submission to God, I _____

_____

_____

_____

_____

_____

6. I know God wants me blessed in every area of my life because

_____

_____

_____

_____

_____

CHAPTER 5

PRAYING GOD'S WORD

I t is the prayer of faith based upon God's Word that will bring results in your life, because the Word of God is the will of God.

How do we get to the point where we can trust God and pray according to His Word? The integrity of God's Word must be established in your heart. You must believe that God said what He meant and meant what He said. You must believe Matthew 24:35: **"Heaven and earth will pass away, but My words will by no means pass away."**

You must get to the point where you believe God's Word more than you believe the 6:00 news, symptoms in your body, the educational process of the world and all the world's facts and figures. You must believe God as the *final authority* in the earth.

The humanist attack the devil has brought against Christianity has been against the integrity of God. The public school systems hammer at it day after day with evolution, which totally rejects God and the Bible account of creation.

It is true that there was a big bang, but it wasn't an accident! It was God's plan. He said, **"'Let there be light'; and there was light"** (Genesis 1:3). He spoke the earth, the firmament, vegetation, the sea creatures, animals and man into existence with the words of His mouth. (See Genesis 1 and 2.)

The enemy has sown seeds into people's minds that the creation story in Genesis isn't true, that man simply started as a one-celled being in a swamp and gradually crawled out like a frog—

from a tadpole to a frog and finally he walked upright. First, he was hunched over, and then he finally straightened up! That is monkey business!

This is why the people who believe this act like monkeys instead of God-inspired creations who walk and talk with God on a daily basis. We're not to have an animal nature. We are built to love, care and share the gospel. It makes sense to believe in God, and all the more when you see the emptiness of people without Him.

Numbers 23:19 says:

> **God is not a man, that He should lie, nor a son of man, that He should repent. Has He said, and will He not do it? Or has He spoken, and will He not make it good?**

First Kings 8:56 says, **"There has not failed one word of all His good promise...."** Not one word of God will ever fail, yet most of men's predictions fail. Some people say the Bible is irrelevant today, but they spend an hour a day reading the newspaper which is so irrelevant it has to be reprinted every day! The things of the world are temporal, but God is eternal. He never changes.

Second Corinthians 1:20 says:

> **For all the promises of God in Him are Yes, and in Him Amen, to the glory of God through us.**

All the religions of the world, except Christianity, have a big "no" on life. But Jesus Christ says "yes" to life, to freedom and liberty, to being everything you are intended to be, to your health, to your needs being met and to going to heaven! All of God's promises are "yes"!

When we settle it that God's Word is true and it is final authority, it isn't hard to pray according to the will of God. But if that is never settled inside of you, you will always be namby pamby, wishy washy in your prayer life.

62

Why Pray God's Word?

Jeremiah 1:12 KJV says, **"I will hasten my word to perform it."** God is committed to fulfill what He has already promised. If He has promised to do something, then He is looking for someone who will believe His Word so He can manifest it.

Second Chronicles 16:9 says:

> **For the eyes of the Lord run to and fro throughout the whole earth, to show Himself strong on behalf of those whose heart is loyal to Him....**

The *King James Translation* of this verse says:

> **For the eyes of the Lord run to and fro throughout the whole earth, to shew himself strong in the behalf of them whose heart is perfect toward him....**

God is waiting for us to believe, speak and act uoon His Word.

Hebrews 4:12-16 KJV says:

> **For the word of God is quick, and powerful, and sharper than any two-edged sword, piercing even to the dividing asunder of soul and spirit, and of the joints and marrow, and is a discerner of the thoughts and intents of the heart.**
>
> **Neither is there any creature that is not manifest in his sight: but all things are naked and opened unto the eyes of him with whom we have to do.**
>
> **Seeing then that we have a great high priest, that is passed into the heavens, Jesus the Son of God, let us hold fast our profession.**
>
> **For we have not an high priest which cannot be touched with the feeling of our infirmities; but was in all points tempted like as we are, yet without sin.**

Let us therefore come boldly unto the throne of grace, that we may obtain mercy, and find grace to help in time of need.

We are to come to the Father in prayer with the promises of His Word. Since the Word is alive and powerful, since Jesus has already gone to heaven and made a way for us and since His blood is on the altar, we can now obtain mercy and grace when we come to the Father in Jesus' name with the Word.

We must establish everything we pray with the Word of God. Second Corinthians 13:1 KJV says, **"In the mouth of two or three witnesses shall every word be established."** If people would take the time to find a promise in God's Word before they offered a petition, they would have a lot more faith when they prayed. One prayer based on the Word of God is more valuable than 10,000 out of your own ideas!

Psalm 37:4 says, **"Delight yourself also in the Lord, and He shall give you the desires of your heart."** He will grant the desires of your heart, but He will also implant His desires into your heart.

How do you know the will of God? Second Timothy 2:15 KJV says, **"Study to shew thyself approved unto God, a workman that needeth not to be ashamed, rightly dividing the word of truth."** As you study God's Word, you will have a revelation of His will for your life.

John 15:7 says:

If you abide in Me, and My words abide in you, you will ask what you desire, and it shall be done for you.

When the Word abides in you and you delight yourself in the Lord, you will pray according to His will.

If you need God's wisdom to know which person to marry, you can pray James 1:5, 1 Corinthians 1:30 and John 10:3,27:

"Jesus, You are made unto me wisdom, and You said that Your sheep hear Your voice. I am Your sheep, and I hear Your voice. I pray and I believe that I receive Your wisdom."

As you pray, God will speak His wisdom inside of your heart. When you pray in line with God's Word, you will pray with accuracy.

Sometimes people have said to me, "Would you agree with me in prayer?" Often, I ask, "What scripture promise are you agreeing with?" Many people aren't aware of the value of praying the promises of God.

Once you have established the integrity of God's Word, you can have confidence that God will fulfill His Word. Some people don't have confidence in their prayer life because they don't have confidence in the Word of God. It's time to clear the doubt and unbelief completely out of your life.

First John 5:14,15 says:

> **Now this is the confidence that we have in Him, that if we ask anything according to His will, He hears us.**
>
> **And if we know that He hears us, whatever we ask, we know that we have the petitions that we have asked of Him.**

In John 15, Jesus teaches on abiding in the Vine. He says, **"For without Me you can do nothing"** (v. 5). That goes for prayer. Apart from the Word of God, apart from a relationship with Jesus Christ, praying for prayer's sake will accomplish nothing.

Pray the Answer

When you pray God's Word, you are praying the answer at the start. Most people's prayer focus is on the problem. They recite the problem with all of its difficulties. They describe it in detail to God as if He doesn't know, and by the time they finish, they have eroded all of their faith, like letting air out of a balloon.

While it is good to commune with the Lord, what really pleases Him is if you will talk about what He has promised to do. "Lord, thank You that You are committed to me. You are El Shaddai, the God Who is more than enough. You are the God of abundance, Jehovah-Jireh. Thank You that You meet all of my needs according to Your riches in glory by Christ Jesus."

Don't you think that sounds more pleasing to God than, "God, this is a bum deal. Where have You been? I can't believe You've left me hanging out on a limb like this. I'm broke, in debt and can't pay my bills. Come on, God."

When people talk that way, how do you think God feels? He has already given His Son and raised Him from the dead. He has already committed all that He has to you.

Sometimes people think, *I'm going to be real honest. I'm just going to tell it like it is.* There are times to get things out of your heart, but the most honest, real thing you can lift up to God is His Word, because it is full of integrity. It will never change. Our thoughts and feelings may change before the sun rises tomorrow, but God never changes, so we can bring the Word in prayer to Him.

Isaiah 55:8,9 says:

> **"For My thoughts are not your thoughts, nor are your ways My ways," says the Lord.**
>
> **"For as the heavens are higher than the earth, so are My ways higher than your ways, and My thoughts than your thoughts."**

If you stopped right there, you could say, "There is no way that we can know the will of God," but Isaiah goes on:

> **"For as the rain comes down, and the snow from heaven, and do not return there, but water the earth, and make it bring forth and bud, that it may give seed to the sower and bread to the eater,**
>
> **"So shall My word be that goes forth from My**

66

mouth; it shall not return to Me void, but it shall accomplish what I please, and it shall prosper in the thing for which I sent it."

Isaiah 55:10,11

We know God's will by His Word and by His Spirit. Colossians 1:9 says, **"That you may be filled with the knowledge of His will in all wisdom and spiritual understanding."**

Isaiah was saying, "The moisture that is in the clouds comes down to the earth in the form of rain. My ways and My thoughts that are in heaven come down upon the earth *in the form of My Word.* As the rain waters the earth and causes it to bring forth, bud, reproduce and multiply, so My Word, when it rains down in your heart, will bring forth My ways, My thoughts and My ideas. I will cause My words and My ways to bud in your life."

Genesis 1 says that every living thing has a seed within itself that will reproduce after its own kind. We see this in the animal kingdom, in the plant kingdom and in humanity. Each reproduces after its own kind. Likewise, God's Word reproduces after its own kind.

The Word of God on salvation will reproduce *salvation.* The Word of God on healing will reproduce *healing.* The Word of God on peace will reproduce *peace.* Begin to pray the promises of God's Word and believe that He is answering and fulfilling His Word on your behalf and on behalf of those for whom you are praying. God is going to fulfill His will in the earth. That's why we should pray, "Lord, Your will be done," when we don't know what the will of God is. Jesus prayed it in the Garden of Gethsemane:

Father, if it is Your will, take this cup away from Me; nevertheless not My will, but Yours, be done.

Luke 22:42

Jesus would be our Substitute, and He would be made a curse

for us. He would die in our place, so He prayed that it would be removed from Him, but He added, *"Nevertheless not My will, but Yours, be done."* We see the humanity and the divinity of Jesus come together when His spirit yielded to the Father's will. Because Jesus was submitted to the divine call, He submitted His body and mind to the Holy Spirit and basically said, "I will do it."

If you know the will of God for your life, then you can pray with authority. For instance, when Jesus came to minister to the sick, you never find one time in Scripture where He lifted His eyes to the Father and said, "Father, *if it be Thy will*, let this blind man be healed." Why? Because Jesus already knew the Father's will was to heal, and He was committed to being an instrument of healing.

The leper questioned God's willingness to heal. He said, **"Lord, if You are willing, You can make me clean"** (Matthew 8:2). He was saying, "I know You've got the ability to heal me, Lord, but are You willing?" Jesus answered, **"I am willing; be cleansed"** (v. 3). The will of God was established in the area of healing. You can know the will of God in every area of life from His Word.

Miss America's Lesson on Prayer

Miss America of 1980—Cheryl Prewitt Salem—was born in a little house on a dirt road in Mississippi. When she was a child, someone passed by her in a country grocery store and said, "Little girl, some day you are going to be Miss America." That word lodged in her heart.

Because of a car accident when Cheryl was eleven years old, one leg was shorter than the other, and she had scars as a result of more than a hundred stitches in her face. It looked like God's plan for her to become Miss America was destroyed, but supernaturally God straightened her leg and removed the scars from her face.

As she won pageant after pageant, Cheryl began to say, "Lord, if You can use me to win Miss Choctaw County, I will do it. If it is Your will, I will do it." She submitted her will to the will of God. In Atlantic City, she prayed the same prayer: "Lord, if You can use me more in this place, I will do it."

After Cheryl won the Miss America 1980 title, she visited our school in Tulsa. Because of her supernatural healing, she had an understanding of the message of faith. She shared her testimony of divine healing every time she had an opportunity to speak.

When Cheryl spoke at our school, she called two little boys forward to illustrate her message. She said to one little boy, "I want you to be the problem," and to the other, "I want you to be the answer." Then she said to the boy who represented the problem, "Any time I start talking about the problem, I want you to get up in my face." She said to the boy who represented the answer, "When I talk about the answer, I want you to get up in my face." She was teaching the students about effective prayer.

Then she began to pray: "Oh, Lord, I've got this terrible problem. I just can't get over it." The little boy who represented the problem got right up in her face, almost nose to nose, and all she could see was the problem.

When you pray the problem and the difficulties, that's all you are going to see. Cheryl couldn't see the answer because the boy representing the problem blocked her vision to everything else.

Then she said, "Lord, I thank You for sending the answer. Thank You for providing for me. Thank You for Your abundance." The problem moved backward, and the answer got right up in her face. As she talked about the answer, all she could see was the answer.

When you pray God's Word, you are praying His will and you are praying the answer. As you pray the answer from God's Word, the problems you face will be swallowed up in victory!

Praying the Answer Brings
the Manifestation

As blind Bartimaeus sat by the road begging and he heard that Jesus of Nazareth was passing by, he cried out, **"Jesus, Son of David, have mercy on me!"** (Mark 10:47). When Jesus asked Bartimaeus, **"What do you want Me to do for you?"** (v. 51), Bartimaeus didn't spend thirty minutes describing how long he had been blind. He didn't take the time to go into all the details of how he lost his sight. He simply responded to Jesus, **"That I may receive my sight"** (v. 51). Jesus said, **"Go your way; your faith has made you well"** (v. 52).

If you will pray the answer—the promises of God from His Word—you will see answers manifest more quickly.

If you are praying for finances, start with Jehovah-Jireh, the God Who sees ahead and makes provision: "My God supplies all of my needs according to His riches in glory by Christ Jesus" (Philippians 4:19).

You can pray the promise of Luke 6:38: "Because I give, it will be given unto me, good measure, pressed down, shaken together and running over will be put into my bosom. For with the same measure I use, it will be measured back to me."

Pray the promise of Psalm 37:25 and Psalm 23:5: "Lord, thank You that I will not be begging bread. Thank You for Your provision. You are the God of abundance. You are El Shaddai, the God Who is more than enough. Thank You that You provide a table for me in the presence of my enemies."

Every time you think about sickness or disease, a problem, or an answer that you need, you can say, "Father, thank You for sending Your answer. Thank You for the provision of it. Thank You that I have it."

How do you handle worry and anxiety? Think about things that are true, honest, just, pure, lovely and of good report (Philippians 4:8).

70

Our church's camp, Camp Victory, came into existence by praying the Word. We searched for a long time for an appropriate place for a camp, and we even did a survey. There was seemingly no way to have our own camp.

You can know God's will by the Word, by the Spirit, by the peace of God, by the inward witness of the Holy Spirit in your spirit, or by something that remains strong in you over a period of time. The counsel of the Lord will stand.

The idea of our own camp was still inside of me, so Sharon and I wrote down: "We want a camp on a lake thirty minutes from Tulsa, with water, sewer, electricity and paved roads." Down at the bottom, I wrote, "For free - Mark 11:24." It came into my heart that I could believe for it, although there was no evidence of a camp in sight! God will give you the desires of your heart. He will give you that which is promised in His Word.

The miracle of Camp Victory happened when we had a phone call from Arles Cole, a member of Victory Christian Center who lives near Keystone Lake. He said, "I have received a call from one of the senators, and he has received contact from the Corps of Engineers. They are looking for a non-profit organization to take over a state park. Would you be interested?"

It was a hundred-acre state park, thirty minutes from downtown Tulsa with water, sewer, electricity and paved roads, and we got it for $1 for every five years that we want to use it. Someone has given the dollar each time we renew!

God will give you the desires of your heart when you delight yourself in Him!

We had a desire in our hearts to reach Spanish-speaking people, so we began to pray, "Lord, help us reach the Spanish-speaking people in our community." God gave us an idea of broadcasting our services in Spanish. Today, we have a large group of Spanish-speaking people in our services who don't understand English. They listen to me preach every service with earphones and transistors because of someone behind the scenes who interprets my message in Spanish. God gave us a way to bring this idea to pass.

If it is God, there will be promises to confirm it in His Word. If you can't find a promise on it, you don't need to be praying it.

At one time, Sharon and I prayed for a van to be used for traveling in ministry. God gave us an opportunity to buy a van in Tulsa at less than the dealer's cost, but I was convinced by someone else that I needed a trailer rather than a van. That was my albatross!

We never slept in the trailer one night, never hooked it up or pulled it once. The miracle is, when I repented and said, "God, forgive me for not going with my spirit," I was able to sell the trailer for what I had in it. Then we prayed, "Lord, we missed the last van. Guide us to the right one."

A short time later when we were in El Dorado, Arkansas, the Lord spoke to me, "Go to the Chevrolet dealership and buy a van." It was a large dealership, and at that time, vans were hot selling vehicles. I walked into the dealership and said, "We want to buy a van." I had just met the owner at a church service.

He said, "I'm sorry, but we've only got one in stock." I said, "We'll take it." He said, "Would you like to see it?" I said, "No, I don't have to see it. We are ready to sign the papers." He said, "Surely you want to get in it and drive it or see it." I said, "If you want us to, we will." Then he said, "I feel to give the van to you at my cost." It's good to hear from the Holy Ghost!

We had prayed and believed that we received, and God had an answer for us! We drove that van for thousands of miles, yet we never had a breakdown, one road problem, or even a flat tire.

Believe You Receive
According to Your Words
A man's stomach shall be satisfied from the

fruit of his mouth; from the produce of his lips he shall be filled.

Death and life are in the power of the tongue, and those who love it will eat its fruit.

Proverbs 18:20,21

Believing that you receive according to what you speak works for life or for death, for positive or for negative, for good or for bad. What are you speaking?

Jesus had something to say about our words, too:

For out of the abundance of the heart the mouth speaks.

A good man out of the good treasure of his heart brings forth good things, and an evil man out of the evil treasure brings forth evil things.

But I say to you that for every idle word men may speak, they will give account of it in the day of judgment

For by your words you will be justified, and by your words you will be condemned.

Matthew 12:34-37

The law of receiving what you speak worked with the children of Israel in Numbers 13 and 14. I'm sure you remember the story. Moses sent twelve men to spy out the land of Canaan God had promised the Israelites.

Ten of the twelve men came back with an evil report of inability to take the land. Only two of the twelve, Joshua and Caleb, came back with a good report: **"Let us go up at once and take possession, for we are well able to overcome it"** (Numbers 13:30). The ten men said **"We are not able to go up against the people, for they are stronger than we"** (v. 31). Though majority opinion in this case was wrong, the Lord said, **"Just as you have spoken in My hearing, so I will do to you"** (Numbers 14 28).

73

Be sure you are speaking what God says!

Hold Fast the Confession of Your Faith

Cast not away therefore your confidence, which hath great recompence of reward.
For ye have need of patience, that, after ye have done the will of God, ye might receive the promise.

Hebrews 10:35,36 KJV

The writer of Hebrews is saying, "Your confident faith will have a great return, but you have need of patience." Some people have a negative connotation of the word *patience*, but Scripture talks about it as "perseverance, endurance, or steadfastness."

Patience undergirds just as a pole, post, or column strengthens a long beam across a building so it won't collapse. Patience and endurance undergird your faith in the time you are standing on the Word, waiting to see the manifestation to your prayers.

Verse 36 in the *New King James Version* says, **"For you have need of endurance, so that after you have done the will of God, you may receive the promise."**

The key is *to do the will of God*, then have patience because you will receive the promise. Don't collapse, don't cave in or become double-minded, but hold fast the confession of your faith, and you will receive God's promises.

God's provision will intersect your obedience. If you stop short in your faith, the provision will be there, but it will be out of your reach. But if you obey, after you have done the will of God, *you will receive the promise!*

What is it you are believing God for? What is it that you need? Don't give up. Don't quit. Find God's promise for it, because it's the promise that God will fulfill. After you have done the will of God, you will receive the promise. So what do you do from prayer to manifestation? Hold fast the confession of your faith!

Your profession (or confession) should go something like this: "Father, I thank You that Your Word is working. Thank You that You meet my every need. Thank You for the manifestation of healing in my body. Thank You, Lord, for all my family being saved and filled with the Holy Spirit. Thank You, Lord, for strength. Thank You for tuition money. Thank You, Father, that I have the mind of Christ. Thank You for redeeming my life from destruction. Thank You, Lord, for giving me a new heart. Thank You for an abundance of Your mercy and grace. I praise You, Lord Jesus. I exalt and magnify You."

The joy of the Lord is your strength. Begin to rejoice in the Word of God. You have believed that you receive, so begin praising the name of Jesus for His answers!

People who don't understand the confession of faith say, "What am I going to do?" You are going to hold fast the confession of your faith. That means you are going to keep your words —all of them—aligned with what God promises you in His Word. Then you are going to praise Him!

Pressure comes to get you off of your confession, and it comes against you in your mind. That's why Jesus said men ought always to pray, and not to faint or lose heart (Luke 18:1). When the circumstances are bad, the problems have been evident for so long, or the difficulties seem so complex, the mind begins to dwell on how tall the giant is instead of how big God is!

With Saul and David, one meditated on the problem and the other meditated on the solution. One hid in fear, and the other went out and whipped the giant! Saul had fainted, but when David came on the scene, the Word inside of him was greater than the words outside of him!

Which report are you going to believe? The report of the Lord Jesus, or the report of the world? The eternal report of the Lord written in His Word is greater than any temporal report of the world!

In the fall of 1973, someone gave me a book about making preparations for the coming economic crash. The author made it sound as if roving mobs of hungry people would be in our streets within a few weeks. It is embarrassing to admit now, but fear got into my heart.

I was learning about trusting God and His Word, but the world's report of economic troubles temporarily overshadowed the Word in my heart.

The author of this book indicated that nuts could be a source of food when all the stores' shelves were empty. It seemed to be wisdom to gather nuts and get a good supply, so I took Sharon down to Woodward Park with two grocery sacks.

That fall was an exceptional year for nuts. We loaded our sacks until we couldn't safely carry any more and then headed for our apartment.

When we got home, I decided to roast some of our precious harvest so we could get a taste of our future diet! Soon our little garage apartment filled with the fragrance of roasting acorns. I cracked one and took a bite. In a flash, a revelation came to me that God must have something better in store for us!

From that time I began to believe that God would be true to His Word and provide abundantly for us. He has honored His Word, and we have left the acorns to the squirrels!

Another incident of having to trust the Word above circumstances occurred when Sharon and I were traveling in ministry.

We were to preach a revival in a small church on the edge of a major city. The pastors of the church were two of the nicest people we encountered in our traveling ministry. As we met them, they said (with a twinkle in their eyes and a chuckle in their voices), "We're going to put you up in the Hilton."

Up until this time, we had stayed mostly in the homes of pastors or church members, so Sharon and I were excited at the thought of staying in a nice hotel. The excitement quickly subsided as they walked us next door to a shotgun row house sitting beside a huge empty field. They gleefully exclaimed, "This is our Hilton."

They explained that there were frequent robberies at the convenience store across the street, but there would be no problem if we stayed in the house when we heard gunshots. They also mentioned that the police often came to the field beside the house to target practice with their guns at night. Again, we were assured there would be no problem if we stayed inside. The final word was that a homeless person often came through the back door and slept in the house. They said he was basically harmless and that he probably would not bother us because it had been some time since his last visit.

Were we going to trust God's Word or be moved by fear? As they walked out of the little house, Sharon and I just looked at each other and then laughed. We would trust God's Word.

It turned chilly that week, and the open gas heater in the center of the room was not vented. The bed was vintage from the early days of the 20th century. The springs were merely lowered with a wire mesh and a sheet. When we crawled into the bed, Sharon and I rolled together in the middle like two hot dogs in a bun!

Trusting God and His Word gave us peace during our stay at the Hilton!

Gospel Prayer Truths

Here are nineteen gospel prayer truths from Chapter 5:

1. The prayer of faith based upon God's Word will bring results in your life, because God hastens to perform His Word (Jeremiah 1:12).

2. To pray effectively, the integrity of God's Word must be established in your own heart.

3. God spoke the earth and everything in it into existence with the words of His mouth (Genesis 1 and 2).

4. God's Word is true, and it is our final authority.

5. Because God's Word is alive and powerful, everything you pray should be aligned with it (Hebrews 4:12).

6. One prayer based on God's Word is more valuable than 10,000 words out of your own intellect.

7. To pray in line with God's Word is to pray with accuracy.

8. To pray God's Word is to pray the answer.

9. God's Word will never return void (Isaiah 55:11).

10. God's ways and His thoughts come from heaven to earth in the form of His Word.

11. God's Word reproduces after its own kind.

12. As you pray the answers you need from God's Word, the problems you face will be swallowed up in victory.

13. God will give you the desires of your heart when you are delighting in Him.

14. You will be satisfied or dissatisfied in life by the words of your own mouth (Proverbs 18:20).

15. Death and life are in the power of your tongue. You are eating the fruit of your own words (Proverbs 18:21).

16. You will be justified or condemned with your own words (Matthews 12:37).

17. Once you have prayed according to God's Word, patience and endurance will carry you through to the full manifestation (Hebrews 10:35,36).

18. Hold fast the confession of your faith, and you will receive God's promises (Hebrews 10:23).

19. God's provision will intersect your obedience.

QUESTIONS

Part 1. Completion

Please complete each of the statements.

1. We can believe in the integrity of God's Word, for Jesus said, "Heaven and earth will pass away, but _____ _____ will by no means pass away" (Matthew 24:35).

2. Numbers 23:19 says, "God is not a man, that He should _____." In other words, what He has spoken, He will do.

3. God says He will _____ to perform His Word in your behalf (Jeremiah 1:12).

4. Everything we pray must be established with the _____ _____ _____.

5. The psalmist David said, "Delight yourself also in the Lord, and He shall give you the _____ of your heart" (Psalm 37:4).

6. Jesus said, "If _____ abide in Me, and _____ _____ abide in you, you will ask what you desire, and it shall be done for you" (John 15:7).

7. To pray with accuracy, pray in line with _____ _____.

8. Proverbs 18:21 says, "_____ and _____ are in the power of the tongue."

9. Jesus said we would be _____ or _____ by our own words (Matthew 12:37).

10. Numbers 14:28 is an admonishment to speak what God says: "Just as you have _____ in My hearing, so I will do to you."

11. _____ which means perseverance, endurance and steadfastness, will undergird your faith while you are waiting for the manifestation of God's promises.

79

12. God's provision will intersect your _____.
13. To hold fast the confession of your faith means to align all your words with God's _____.
14. The _____ report of the Lord written in His Word is greater than any temporal report of the world.

Part 2. Personal Application

Please complete the questions and/or statements to the best of your ability.

1. Because I delight myself in the Lord, He will _____

   _____

2. The continual input of God's Word in my life is _____

   _____

   _____

   _____

3. To assure that "life" rather than "death" comes off of my tongue, as Proverbs 18:21 states, I am _____

   _____

   _____

   _____

   _____

4. Once I have prayed God's Word, I will _____

   _____

   _____

   _____

   _____

CHAPTER 6

PRAYING THE WORD AMISS

W hen God directs you to do something, then you will have faith to do it. This is what I call "Spirit-directed faith."

Abraham didn't say, "I think it's about time I leave Ur of the Chaldees. This place is getting shabby and run down. I think I'll go to Palestine." No! God initiated the call to Abraham. When we talk about the faith of Abraham, he had something to base it on, because God already had spoken. I call it "Spirit-directed faith."

It's the same way with Elijah. He could say it wasn't going to rain for three and a half years because God had spoken to him. Though Elijah had faith, it was out of response to what God had already said that he prayed and reaped the exact manifestation of what he spoke in prayer.

In the fall of 1992, we had 49 days to come up with $1.5 million to purchase the former Oral Roberts Evangelistic Association building. People said it was a miracle to be able to purchase the building in such a short time period. We had to have faith, but the key was: *God spoke it.* We aren't running the show. God is in management, and we are in sales! He directs us, and we just follow through and hold fast the confession of our faith.

Faith comes by hearing God's Word, and many people think that just means the written Word. God is still talking, so it also means we have faith to do what He speaks to us to do.

When I transferred to Oral Roberts University mid-term of my sophomore year, leaving a full-college scholarship at a state college in Arkansas, I didn't get my directive from Genesis or Exodus! God spoke it to me, and I obeyed. I went through the remaining two and a half years at O.R.U. debt free because I had faith for what God had spoken.

When God spoke to build our facilities across from the O.R.U. campus, I had faith for it because He spoke it. Anything He speaks will always agree with the Word. It will never be contradictory or in violation of the Word or the principles and counsel of the Word. God is still speaking, and when you have the word of the Lord, then you can act.

Many people who have criticized the word of faith have either not heard accurately or they are swayed in their beliefs because of people who have misrepresented faith. In most cases, people have not heard correctly. People who are critical of the faith message often say, "You can say whatever you want to, and it will come to pass. Just speak it, and it will come to pass." That is not true. *When God speaks*, then we speak it and it comes to pass. What God says, we can say and it will be fulfilled.

Faith is prompted by the Spirit of the Lord. *Logos* is that which the Spirit has written, as opposed to *rhema*, that which is spoken under the anointing of the Holy Spirit.

Let's look at a couple of illustrations to clarify what I am saying about the confession of the Word. Isaiah 7:14 says a **"virgin shall conceive...."** An unmarried woman could start confessing this Scripture, but it would be ridiculous because God's Spirit spoke it only to Mary. It was a word just for her.

Other people have gotten in the ditch about Judas. The Bible says after Judas betrayed innocent blood (Jesus' blood) and threw down the thirty pieces of silver in the temple he had been given for his part in the conspiracy, he **"went and hanged himself"** (Matthew 27:5). Luke 10:37 says, **"Go and do likewise."** God's Spirit isn't telling you to go and hang yourself as Judas did, but both of these verses are in the Bible. They were accurately recorded, but you can't pull Scripture out of context and receive an accurate account of what is being spoken.

Judas violated God's principles and desecrated his own life by selling the Son of God to crucifixion. What happened to him was the result of his own actions. You can learn by Judas' life, but this certainly isn't something you want to confess over your own life. This is why we must "rightly divide" the Word of God. We need the anointing of the Holy Spirit to know what God is speaking to us.

I remember a situation where a young lady sat near a young man in class. They developed a friendly relationship during the breaks between classes. She began to confess, "Father, I believe that I receive this man for my husband. Thank You that he will be my husband."

One day the young man walked into class with another young lady. He said, "I would like for you to meet my wife. She is off work today and was able to come to class." The female classmate was confessing, naming and claiming this married man to be her husband, and that's exactly why criticism of the faith message has come. God's Word has to be directed by the Spirit of the Lord; otherwise, you will claim things out of your own fleshly desires.

James said, **"Ye ask, and receive not, because ye ask amiss, that ye may consume it upon your lusts"** (James 4:3 KJV). The key thing to discern is, *"What is the will of God?"*

I recall another situation where a young man, about 24 years old, married and the father of one young child, began to boldly confess, "In three years, I am going to have a ministry equivalent to Kenneth Copeland's." I tried to convey to this guy that we're not to compare ourselves with other people, but we are called to be servants. If God wants us to be in a high profile, that's His decision—not ours. This young man was under the delusion of pursuing fame.

Other people pursue fortune, power, position and prestige by speaking portions of the Word erroneously. It is sad to take the message that saves, delivers and heals and pervert it to cause a bad report in the world. Just because a few people have done some ridiculous things, however, doesn't mean we are to give up on believing and speaking the Word of God. That which is spoken in line with the Word of God will come to pass for good in our lives.

Gospel Prayer Truths

Here are five gospel prayer truths from Chapter 6:

1. Spirit-directed faith is birthed out of God prompting you to do something.

2. Put faith with what God has spoken, and you will see the manifestation of it.

3. What God speaks by His Spirit will always agree with His Word.

4. The key motivation for effective prayer is to discern God's will (James 4:3).

5. That which you speak in line with God's Word will come to pass for good in your life.

QUESTIONS

Part 1. Completion

Please complete each of the statements.

1. Faith comes by _____ God's Word repeatedly (Romans 10:17).

2. Anything God speaks will always agree with His _____.

3. _____ refers to the written Word, while _____ refers to the spoken Word.

4. In James 4:3 KJV, the reason James gives why Christians ask in prayer but do not receive is they ask _____, which means they ask from wrong motives or to satisfy their own lusts and desires.

Part 2. Personal Application

Please complete the questions and/or statements to the best of your ability.

1. My primary motive behind my prayers for others is _____

   _____

   _____

   _____

2. The primary motive behind prayer for specific areas of my own life is _____

   _____

   _____

   _____

CHAPTER 7

USING THE NAME OF
JESUS IN PRAYER

The name of Jesus is the name above all names. No other name is higher than the name of Jesus. The name of Jesus is your key to heaven's storehouse. It is the key that unlocks all the blessings of God.

The privilege to use the name of Jesus in prayer comes out of a proper relationship with Him. We are to speak in His name as His instrument in response to His directives.

Jesus said:

> **"Most assuredly, I say to you, he who believes in Me, the works that I do he will do also; and greater works than these he will do, because I go to My Father."**
>
> **John 14:12**

I believe one of those greater works today is that we have the privilege to preach Jesus Christ and see people born again. Jesus multiplied the loaves and fishes, calmed the storms, raised the dead, caused maimed limbs to grow out and withered hands and paralytics to be healed and brought deliverance to the demon-possessed and the mentally deranged.

In speaking to those *who were in relationship with Him*, Jesus said:

> **"And whatever you ask in My name, that I will do, that the Father may be glorified in the Son.**
>
> **"If you ask anything in My name, I will do it."**
>
> **John 14:13,14**

Submission to Authority
Releases Authority to You

I believe people have flippantly used the name of Jesus without having a proper relationship with Him. What happened to the seven sons of Sceva is a good example of this.

Then some of the itinerant Jewish exorcists took it upon themselves to call the name of the Lord Jesus over those who had evil spirits, saying, "We exorcise you by the Jesus whom Paul preaches."

Also there were seven sons of Sceva, a Jewish chief priest, who did so.

And the evil spirit answered and said, "Jesus I know, and Paul I know; but who are you?"

Then the man in whom the evil spirit was leaped on them, overpowered them, and prevailed against them, so that they fled out of that house naked and wounded.

Acts 19:13-16

Apparently the seven sons of Sceva had seen or heard of miracles as a result of using the name of Jesus, and they said, "Let's try it." They "tried" using Jesus' name with a man who had an evil spirit.

The key to the defeat of the seven sons of Sceva by one man possessed of a devil was: They used the right formula, they used the right words, but they were not "in" the name of Jesus, meaning, *personally, they weren't in relationship with Jesus Christ.* Because of having no viable relationship with Jesus, they were literally using the name of Jesus in vain. To them, the name of Jesus was merely a catch word.

If you are *in* the name of Jesus, the devil knows who you are. If you're not *in* His name, he also knows who you are. The devil knew that the seven sons of Sceva didn't have the authority that

Paul had in the name of Jesus. Authority is based on being under authority.

When the Roman centurion came to Jesus to seek healing for his servant, he said to Jesus:

> **"Lord, my servant is lying at home paralyzed, dreadfully tormented."**
>
> **And Jesus said to him, "I will come and heal him."**
>
> **The centurion answered and said, "Lord, I am not worthy that You should come under my roof. But only speak a word, and my servant will be healed.**
>
> **"For I also am a man under authority, having soldiers under me. And I say to this one, 'Go,' and he goes; and to another, 'Come,' and he comes; and to my servant, 'Do this,' and he does it."**
>
> **When Jesus heard it, He marveled, and said to those who followed, "Assuredly, I say to you, I have not found such great faith, not even in Israel!"**
>
> **Matthew 8:6-10**

How did the Roman centurion have what Jesus called "great faith"? He had it because he was under authority. He had been given authority, and he understood authority.

If you understand that God has authority and you submit to His authority, then you will receive the delegated authority Jesus has given you as a believer. The seven sons of Sceva were not *in* the name of Jesus. They had no authority in Jesus' name because they weren't under His authority.

Abiding in the Word

To abide in Jesus Christ is to abide in God's Word. John 15:7 puts this scriptural principle in an even clearer light:

89

"If you abide in Me, and My words abide in you, you will ask what you desire, and it shall be done for you."

To be *in the name of Jesus* is to be in the Word of God. According to Psalm 138:2, God's Word is magnified above His name.

If you are going to relate to the name of Jesus, you have to be identified with the Word of God—abiding in it, dwelling in it, walking in it, submitted to it and committed to obeying *all* of it. Some people want to obey only the parts which please them.

On a return flight from one of the crusades we held in St. Petersburg, Russia, I awoke after a few hours of sleep and saw a man watching me. He said, "I noticed you've got a big Bible. My father gave me one, but I haven't read it. I've been thinking about it, but I wanted to talk to someone about it first."

He said, "Life is so full of distractions." Even though he had had several drinks, I read portions of the Bible to him. He would say, "I'll take that."

Then I read to him from John 3:15-21:

Whoever believes in Him should not perish but have eternal life.

For God so loved the world that He gave His only begotten Son, that whoever believes in Him should not perish but have everlasting life.

For God did not send His Son into the world to condemn the world, but that the world through Him might be saved.

He who believes in Him is not condemned; but he who does not believe is condemned already, because he has not believed in the name of the only begotten Son of God.

And this is the condemnation, that the light has come into the world, and men loved darkness rather than light, because their deeds were evil.

For everyone practicing evil hates the light and does not come to the light, lest his deeds should be exposed.

But he who does the truth comes to the light, that his deeds may be clearly seen, that they have been done in God.

He accepted the part about God loves you, but when we got to the part about **"men loved darkness rather than light, because their deeds were evil,"** he started slapping the Bible and said, "No, no, I don't want that."

We must accept *all* of God's Word, not just parts of it. We're talking about being *in the name*. We're talking about being immersed and submitted to all of God's Word. Commit to the light that you have. Submit to what you understand of the Lord. Then, as you grow in Him, you should make deeper commitments.

If you are delighting in the Lord, that means you are delighting in the Word of God. If you are feasting in God's Word, then you will have right desires that are in agreement with the Word. You will be able to discern and divide. The Word divides between the soul and the spirit, and you will be able to see whether a desire is soulish and selfish—out of your mind and emotions—or out of your spirit which is dominated by the Holy Spirit.

Psalm 119:130 AMP says of God's Word:

The entrance and unfolding of Your words give light; their unfolding gives understanding (discernment and comprehension) to the simple.

The entrance of God's Word into your mind and heart brings light. It divides so that you can ask anything in the name of Jesus. When you are hooked into the name of Jesus, you are abiding in the Word of God, and you have surrendered your life to the Lord, trusting Him in every area of your life.

91

Bring Forth Fruit That Will Remain

You did not choose Me, but I chose you and appointed you that you should go and bear fruit, and that your fruit should remain, that whatever you ask the Father in My name He may give you.

John 15:16

Jesus is speaking of the *authority in His name*. The fruit He desires is *answered prayer*. The fruit of the Spirit is love, joy, peace, longsuffering, kindness, goodness, faithfulness, gentleness and self-control (Galatians 5:22,23). In John 15:16 KJV Jesus said, **"I have chosen you, and ordained you, that ye should go and bring forth fruit, and that your fruit should remain...."**

We are to bear many kinds of fruit. The fruit that will remain is fruit that is birthed by prayer in the name of Jesus.

What you bring forth by your own abilities, you can take the credit for, but if you have asked for it in Jesus' name, then the Father will be glorified when the prayer is answered, such as with souls being saved.

Years ago, I led a young man to Christ who was on drugs and alcohol. He started coming to our youth group. His parents were going to Bible school to be trained in ministry. They had just come out of the secular world and were turned on to God. Because of the lifestyle they had lived, however, their kids were still in the same junk they had been involved in.

Their son often came into the youth group high on drugs and alcohol. He would sit in the back and make fun of what we were doing, mocking us as we praised the Lord and talking while we shared. Although he was bigger than me, about 6'2" and 200 pounds, I got hold of him one time and said, "You be quiet, and you sit down."

One night, we decided to have a prayer meeting and fellowship at our house. This young man showed up for two reasons: food and girls. He had his own afterglow planned—a six pack in his car.

We were sitting in a little circle in the living room, and someone asked for prayer for one of his relatives who was going through a real struggle. As we began to pray, the Spirit of God manifested Himself in that room.

Greg sat by the door where he could get out whenever he wanted to leave. As I knelt beside him to pray for the person who asked for prayer, the Lord said, "Lay your hand on Greg's knee." It happened so fast he didn't have time to escape!

As my hand touched Greg's knee, the power of God fell, and Greg started to weep. He gave his life to Christ, was baptized in the Holy Spirit and committed his life to the ministry that night. We literally danced in the front yard at midnight because of the breakthrough in Greg's life.

Greg went to Bible school to be trained for the ministry and became a youth pastor in Colorado. A few years after Greg started in ministry, he called me and said, "Your fruit remains." Today, Greg and Lisa Glassford are ministering to young people all over the country with books, tapes, singing, preaching and seminars.

In John 16:23,24, Jesus said:

> **And in that day you will ask Me nothing. Most assuredly, I say to you, whatever you ask the Father in My name He will give you.**
>
> **Until now you have asked nothing in My name. Ask, and you will receive, that your joy may be full.**

Think of it. Jesus, the Son of God, walked with the disciples every day. Anything they had need of, they could ask for. When there wasn't anything to feed the multitude, Jesus took a little boy's sack lunch and fed 5,000 with it. When there was a storm and the disciples were about to sink, Jesus stopped it with the words of His mouth. Whatever they needed, He was there to provide it.

In these verses, Jesus was telling the disciples that He was going to leave them, but He assured them that He would send the Comforter Who would guide them into all truth. Jesus would give them His name to use after He was crucified, resurrected and ascended to the Father. With His name, the disciples could go directly into the Throne Room of the Father. Today, we can go directly into the presence of the Father, too, simply by using the name of Jesus.

Jesus said, **"Ask, and you will receive, that your joy may be full"** (John 16:24). Fullness of joy comes when you receive answers to prayer. When Greg came to Christ, we had joy unspeakable and full of glory! We had been praying to the Father in the name of Jesus on Greg's behalf.

How Did Jesus Get His Name?

Jesus got His name in three ways: obedience, resurrection and inheritance.

First, *Jesus received His name and the power that's in it by obedience.*

> **Let this mind be in you which was also in Christ Jesus,**
>
> **Who, being in the form of God, did not consider it robbery to be equal with God,**
>
> **But made Himself of no reputation, taking the form of a bondservant, and coming in the likeness of men.**
>
> **And being found in appearance as a man, He humbled Himself and became obedient to the point of death, even the death of the cross.**
>
> **Therefore God also has highly exalted Him and**

given Him the name which is above every name,

That at the name of Jesus every knee should bow, of those in heaven, and of those on earth, and of those under the earth,

And that every tongue should confess that Jesus Christ is Lord, to the glory of God the Father.

Philippians 2:5-11

One of the boys in the youth group I was pastoring had come home from school one afternoon, looked out the window and saw a tornado approaching his parent's home. He had been hearing the Word of God, and he said, "Mr. Devil, you get your tornado out of here *in the name of Jesus.*" The tornado cloud that was quickly approaching his parent's home lifted back up into the clouds. What a mighty God we serve! There's authority in the name of Jesus.

Every tongue will confess Jesus Christ as Lord, whether in this life or in the next, whether in heaven or in hell. The best time to do it is in this life through salvation—accepting Jesus Christ as your Lord and Savior.

Second, *Jesus got His name by the resurrection from the dead.*

And what is the exceeding greatness of His power toward us who believe, according to the working of His mighty power

Which He worked in Christ when He raised Him from the dead and seated Him at His right hand in the heavenly places,

Far above all principality and power and might and dominion, and every name that is named, not only in this age but also in that which is to come.

And He put all things under His feet, and gave Him to be head over all things to the church,

95

Which is His body, the fullness of Him who fills all in all.

Ephesians 1:19-23

The name of Jesus is above everything that has a name. It is above sickness and disease, poverty and lack and anything else that has a name!

Third, *Jesus got His name and the power in His name through inheritance.*

"He has by inheritance obtained a more excellent name than they" (Hebrews 1:4). That means the name of Jesus is more excellent than the angels, any human being, or any demon spirit. Just as you got your name from your parents, Jesus inherited His name, a royal name, from His Father.

Power of Attorney in Jesus' Name

You and I, as believers in the Lord Jesus Christ, have been given the power of attorney in Jesus' name. In legal terminology, we have been given authority to act for Jesus Christ by using His name.

Jesus said of His followers, which includes you and me:

And these signs will follow those who believe: In My name they will cast out demons; they will speak with new tongues;

They will take up serpents; and if they drink anything deadly, it will by no means hurt them; they will lay hands on the sick, and they will recover.

Mark 16:17,18

Jesus was saying, "Everything I have been doing, you will do." It's called, "Carry on business as usual in My name."

If you are going to go somewhere and you want business to go on as usual, you can confer upon another person the right to sign checks, enter into contracts, receive goods, negotiate business and carry on whatever needs to be done, if you specify it in a legal document. When you are gone, your name can be used by the designated person to whom you have given the legal power of attorney.

Jesus was saying, "While I'm gone, you take My name and heal the sick, raise the dead, cleanse the lepers and cast out devils. Demonstrate My authority. When you are vitally linked into My name, you are abiding in the Word, you have submitted your life and surrendered it under My authority, then *whatever you ask the Father in My name, I will do it*. You will be acting in My stead."

The power of attorney is legalized spiritually in us when Jesus abides in us through the Person of the Holy Spirit. We can't just take His name. We are *in* His name. We have wrapped our lives in His name. We have surrendered and submitted to His name. Therefore, when we take the name of Jesus and lay hands on someone in that name, we break the power of homosexuality, drug addiction, immorality, alcoholism, uncleanness, perversion and any other form of evil.

God is saying, "I will use My power to bring to pass the words that you speak when you are operating in My will in accordance with My Word, in Jesus' name."

Gospel Prayer Truths

Here are eight gospel prayer truths from Chapter 7:

1. The name of Jesus is your key to all of God's blessings.
2. The privilege of using Jesus' name in prayer comes out of a proper relationship with Him.
3. Authority is based on being under authority. When you are under God's authority, you will receive the authority Jesus has delegated to you as a believer.
4. To be "*in* the name of Jesus" is to be "in the Word of God"—immersed in the Word and submitted to *all* of it.

97

5. To "bring forth fruit" is to see the manifestation of the answers to your prayers, such as souls being saved.

6. The name of Jesus is above everything that has a name.

7. As a born-again believer in Jesus Christ, you have been given the power of attorney to use Jesus' name in prayer.

8. Every believer is to demonstrate God's authority in the earth by healing the sick, raising the dead and casting out devils, in Jesus' name.

QUESTIONS

Part 1. Completion

Please complete each of the statements.

1. The name above all names, in heaven, in the earth and under the earth is the name of _____.

2. Jesus said in John 14:14, "If you ask anything in _____ _____, I will do it." He is speaking to everyone who is in relationship with Him.

3. The centurion had what Jesus called "great faith," because he was a man submitted to _____.

4. God's _____ _____ is magnified above Jesus' name (Psalm 138:2).

5. The entrance of God's Word into your mind and heart brings _____ (Psalm 119:130).

6. Jesus' desire is that all believers bear fruit that will remain (John 15:16). The fruit He is referring to is that which is birthed in _____.

7. In what three ways did Jesus get His name?

    a. _____

    b. _____

    c. _____

8. Jesus "made Himself of no reputation, taking the form of a _____, and coming in the likeness of men" (Philippians 2:7).

9. Because Jesus " _____ Himself and became _____ to the point of death...God...highly exalted Him and [gave] Him the name which is above _____ _____ " (Philippians 2:8,9).

10. As believers, we have been given the name of Jesus to

99

demonstrate His _____ in the earth by healing the sick, cleansing the lepers (those with incurable diseases), raising the dead and casting out devils.

11. The power of attorney is legalized spiritually in us when Jesus abides in us through the Person of the _____

   _____.

Part 2. Personal Application

Please complete the questions and/or statements to the best of your ability.

1. I have power and authority in the name of Jesus because

   _____

   _____

   _____

   _____

2. To me, Jesus' name means _____

   _____

   _____

   _____

   _____

3. I am bringing forth fruit that will remain for God's Kingdom by _____

   _____

   _____

   _____

   _____

CHAPTER 8
THE PRAYER OF AGREEMENT

There is awesome power when you come into agreement with other believers in prayer. We know that one can put a thousand to flight, but two can put ten thousand to flight (Deuteronomy 32:30).

In the natural, when people combine their efforts in work, what they accomplish corporately is far greater than what they can do individually. The multiplication factor enters into it. It's the same in prayer as in business. Corporations can do the same thing with their impact when they are flowing together in agreement and in cooperation with others. Many times their profit margin and impact on certain markets can be multiplied by a corporate effort.

The foundation for the prayer of agreement is found in Matthew 18:15-20.

> **Moreover if your brother sins against you, go and tell him his fault between you and him alone. If he hears you, you have gained your brother.**
>
> **Verse 15**

What is the goal of telling someone their fault? To tell them off, set them straight, or knock them back a lick? No! It's to gain your brother or sister, because if there has been an offense against you, then there is a breach or a breakdown—a place where the enemy can come in.

Notice, Jesus says the *first step* in resolving a difficulty is to go to the person *alone*. It doesn't say, "Talk to your best friend about it. Confide in your husband or wife about it. Confide in your minister about it." It says, "Go and talk with that person *alone.*"

Many of the world's problems, difficulties in relationships, negotiation breakdowns and problems in churches and families would be resolved if this step were taken. When the objective is reconciliation and restoration, then the attitude that comes across will produce an atmosphere where reconciliation and restoration are possible. The attitude is so important. When you go to someone and say, "You're wrong, buddy," do you think there will be a reconciliation? It's not likely! But if you approach it by asking, "Could you explain to me what happened?" or "Why did this take place?" you create an atmosphere free of hostility where restoration can take place.

Some people's greatest exercise is jumping to conclusions, running down their neighbors and pitching a fit. Make an effort to get the facts. Some people spend their lives being upset or angry with people, which will eat away at them like a cancer. "Go to the person alone" is a prelude Jesus gives to the prayer of agreement.

> **But if he will not hear you, take with you one or two more, that "by the mouth of two or three witnesses every word may be established."**
>
> **Matthew 18:16**

The principle of two or three witnesses, found in both the Old and New Testaments, is to establish or verify something. This doesn't mean to go and get your two meanest, biggest friends. I believe it means to go with two people who are objective and who will hear and understand both sides.

I have found at times in counseling people with marriage problems, that when the wife tells her side of the story, you wonder why the husband is allowed to live. Then, when the husband shares his side of the story, you wonder if this is the same man! There also is a difference when you hear people tell something in private and when you have them tell it in front of someone. It's amazing how stories change!

A person who has a chip on his shoulder or an emotional need in his life may receive something that is said or done with a wrong attitude when nothing is meant by it.

In the world, the principle of using two or three witnesses is called arbitration. All parties agree to a group of people who will objectively hear both sides, and they agree to abide by the decision of that group.

This is what Jesus was teaching. Take your difficulties before two or three other people, and let them help you understand it. Then either or both parties should make any necessary adjustments.

> **And if he refuses to hear them, tell it to the church. But if he refuses even to hear the church, let him be to you like a heathen and a tax collector.**
>
> **Matthew 18:17**

This doesn't mean that every Sunday morning we should hear all the grievances before the entire church congregation. This would make the church a courtroom, and it would destroy the anointing in the service. I believe Jesus is talking about the leadership of the church. In other words, tell it to the representative leader of the church to whom you are submitted.

In our church, if there is a challenge in a particular area, it is brought before those who are in spiritual authority over the particular area involved. If someone refuses to be reconciled, then they are acting in unforgiveness, and in the spirit of unforgiveness, they are acting like an unsaved person. Saved people are forgivers!

Jesus said, **"But if he refuses even to hear the church, let him be to you like a heathen and a tax collector"** (Matthew 18:17). Does that mean you are going to trample on them and talk ugly about them? No! When an unsaved person treats you wrong, *pray for them*. Bless those who persecute you. Pray for those who despitefully use you. Your prayers will be hindered if you don't deal with unresolved conflict with others.

This is what Peter dealt with in 1 Peter 3:1-7:

> **Wives, likewise, be submissive to your own husbands, that even if some do not obey the word, they, without a word, may be won by the conduct of their wives,**
>
> **When they observe your chaste conduct accompanied by fear.**
>
> **Do not let your adornment be merely outward—arranging the hair, wearing gold, or putting on fine apparel—**
>
> **Rather let it be the hidden person of the heart, with the incorruptible beauty of a gentle and quiet spirit, which is very precious in the sight of God.**
>
> **For in this manner, in former times, the holy women who trusted in God also adorned themselves, being submissive to their own husbands,**
>
> **As Sarah obeyed Abraham, calling him lord, whose daughters you are if you do good and are not afraid with any terror.**
>
> **Husbands, likewise, dwell with them with understanding, giving honor to the wife, as to the weaker vessel, and as being heirs together of the grace of life, that your prayers may not be hindered.**

Treating people wrong and not reconciling relationships will break down the power of your prayer life. I have heard people say, "I have prayed and confessed the Word. I am tithing. Why isn't it working?" Usually I ask, "Have you checked your love life? Are you walking in love toward other people? Have you reconciled your differences?" Just because someone is mad at you doesn't mean you have to be mad at them, or just because someone is having an argument doesn't mean you have to have one with them. It can be a one-sided deal. Make every effort to reconcile.

Follow the steps Jesus gave:
1. Go to the offender *alone*.
2. If he/she will not hear you, take one or two objective people with you.
3. Then, if the offender refuses to listen, go to the proper leadership in the church.

Then pray for the offender: "Lord, I forgive, release and bless _____. I want this completely out of my spirit. Every time I think about _____, I am going to thank You that You are working in them." In this way, you protect your own spirit.

Proverbs 4:23 says, **"Keep your heart with all diligence, for out of it spring the issues of life."** The issues or forces of life are love, joy, peace, longsuffering, kindness, goodness, faithfulness, gentleness and self-control (Galatians 5:22,23).

Protect your spirit, for out of it flow the fruit of the Holy Spirit. If your spirit is clogged up with unforgiveness, bitterness and resentment, then the fruit won't flow as freely as it should. Love, joy and faith won't flow freely, so you stand to lose your joy, get out of love and stop the effectiveness of your faith because your relationships with people have broken down.

I want to encourage you. It doesn't matter what other people have done. You can reconcile on your side of the fence! Hebrews 12:14 says, **"Pursue peace with all people...."** Pray that even your enemies will be reconciled to you. Proverbs 16:7 says, **"When a man's ways please the Lord, He makes even his enemies to be at peace with him."**

Offenses will come, but how you deal with them is what determines what will happen in your life. Deal with them with God's grace.

Joseph couldn't be stopped from reaching the highest promotion God had planned for him, in spite of three major offenses in his life. His brothers sold him, he was maliciously slandered by Potiphar's wife and he ended up in prison.

In Genesis 50:20, Joseph summed up the whole ordeal:

But as for you, you meant evil against me; but God meant it for good, in order to bring it about as it is this day, to save many people alive.

What God has planned for you cannot be stopped by what other people do against you. Joseph could not be stopped because he kept on forgiving. He kept rising to the top. He rose to the top in Potiphar's house, and they put him down. At the bottom of the prison, he rose to the top again. And then forgotten, he rose to the top from prison to prime minister in one day. Glory to God!

When someone offends you, you cannot stay in neutral. If you do, the offense stays in you. But if you'll go the second mile joyfully and turn the other cheek, then you have actually planted a seed of love into that person's life.

At one point in our ministry, Sharon and I received a devastating letter from a couple who used to attend our church. They attacked everything we had ever done. We prayed Proverbs 16:7: "Lord, You said if our ways please You, You will make even our enemies be at peace with us."

A few days after receiving the letter, I called the person who wrote the letter. As he went through one thing after another, I tried to respond in such a way as to let him know that we loved him and cared about him. By the end of the conversation, he said, "We love you all so much, we are praying for you and we believe the whole ministry is going to work for good."

We get calls or letters every week from someone who is bent out of shape over something. If your hide is not tough and your heart full of love, you won't last in the ministry. Years ago, I asked Dr. Roy Hicks, former superintendent of the Four Square

Gospel Churches, "If you could tell us one thing to help us to be successful in ministry, what would it be?" We were ready to go on the road in a traveling ministry.

Dr. Hicks' response was, "If you don't get bitter, you will make it." He hit the nail on the head! The primary thing that we have seen move people out of marriage, out of churches and out of ministry is bitterness. People forget to practice the principles Jesus gave for reconciliation in Matthew 18.

Many times when people strike out at you, they've got a problem in some area of their life, and you just happen to be the scapegoat—the one who gets hit with it. People who are bitter do strike out. That's just a fact. They have hurts in their lives, but we are called to heal bitter waters. At the waters of Marah, God showed Moses a tree to cast into those waters and make them sweet (Exodus 15:23-25). We still have that tree! It's called Calvary—the cross where we die to ourselves and we lift up Jesus Christ!

Binding and Loosing

Jesus said:

Assuredly, I say to you, whatever you bind on earth will be bound in heaven, and whatever you loose on earth will be loosed in heaven.

Matthew 18:18

What is Jesus talking about? He just got through dealing with forgiveness and reconciliation. Now He's talking about binding and loosing. Many of us have been taught verse 18 out of context. In context, when you forgive people on the earth, you loose the power of heaven upon their lives. When you don't forgive or reconcile with them on earth, you stop the power of God from ministering to them.

Reconciliation and restoration are loosed when you forgive someone, but people are bound by an offense when an attitude of unforgiveness prevails.

When I was a student at Oral Roberts University, I met a young man named Paul. He had a boyhood friend who was very bright, handsome, strong and athletic, but always put himself down. Paul, thinking this was really "cool," would say the same kinds of things about himself. The result in Paul's life was self-condemnation and severe depression. Both went their separate ways. Paul had given his life to Jesus and ended up at O.R.U. where I met him. The friend was not a Christian.

One night at vespers, Paul was feeling very depressed about his life so he went out to the Prayer Gardens on campus to ask the Lord what was wrong with his life. He was reminded of his friend and how that relationship caused him to say the wrong things about himself, resulting in the state of depression he currently found himself in. Paul came to the realization that he needed to forgive his friend and right there in the garden he said, "Lord, forgive me and I forgive, release and bless _____."

As Paul left the service, he returned to his dorm. At that time, we only had one phone in the dorm lobby and students would collect their messages as they came in. When Paul walked into his dorm, he found a message to return a call to someone whose name he didn't even recognize because of the spelling of the name. When he called the number on the message note, he realized it was his friend! He had called him to tell him what had been going on in his life—drugs, alcohol, etc.—but that he had just accepted Jesus Christ. The only person he wanted to tell was Paul, whom he had not seen in several years.

Whatever you loose in the earth is loosed in the heavenlies. There is power in what we do in the earth with forgiveness.

The setting of Luke 6:36-38 is forgiveness:

Therefore be merciful, just as your Father also is merciful.

Judge not, and you shall not be judged. Condemn not, and you shall not be condemned. Forgive, and you will be forgiven.

> **Give, and it will be given to you: good measure,**
> **pressed down, shaken together, and running over will**
> **be put into your bosom. For with the same measure**
> **that you use, it will be measured back to you.**

In the way you give, it will be given back to you. Show mercy and mercy will be released into your life and into the lives of others.

In Matthew 18:19, 20, Jesus is still speaking in the context of forgiveness and reconciliation.

> **Again I say to you that if two of you agree on**
> **earth concerning anything that they ask, it will be**
> **done for them by My Father in heaven.**

> **For where two or three are gathered together in**
> **My name, I am there in the midst of them.**

Agreement is more than simply saying to someone, "Agree with me." It is agreement in the Spirit. Are you in agreement with the Lord? You can't have the power of God working in your life if you aren't in agreement with God. What does that mean? If you are in bitterness and resentment, you aren't in agreement with Jesus. Before you agree with another person, agree with Jesus Christ, and make sure your spirit is in agreement with God's Word and His will.

When you really want the power of agreement with another person, you need someone whose spirit is flowing with your spirit, so you don't simply come into a mental agreement. You need to have a spiritual heart agreement.

I believe the reason there is such a great attack on marriages is that there is no other agreement on the face of the earth more powerful than that of a husband and wife. Two people in perfect agreement with the Spirit of God make a three-fold cord, and Ecclesiastes 4:12 says, **"A threefold cord is not quickly broken."**

As a person planted seed in Victory's building fund toward the fulfillment of their own vision, they asked me to come into agreement with them for their vision. I said, "I don't have your vision, and God hasn't spoken to me about what you are to do, but *I can agree with you in my spirit for the will of God to be done.*"

When you don't know specific information that may be needed to come into prayer agreement with someone, you can always agree for the will of the Lord to be done.

The Power of Agreement Used in a Negative Way

In Genesis 11:6, the power of agreement worked in a negative way when the people determined they were going to build a tower to reach up to heaven. The Lord had to stop them, so He came down and confused their languages.

And the Lord said, "Indeed the people are one and they all have one language, and this is what they begin to do; now nothing that they propose to do will be withheld from them."

They had one mind, one language and one vision. They weren't saved, nor were they building the tower for God, yet God was saying, "There is power in their human ability that whatever they set their hand to do, they are going to do it unless I stop them." God stopped them because it was an agreement of evil.

In the natural realm, great feats have been accomplished in corporate structures when there has been agreement. God created man to have dominion in the earth, and in some cases, man has taken that power and perverted it or defaulted in its use. God's original plan was that man would have dominion to bring the earth under control for His glory.

The building of the tower of Babel reveals to us the power of unity. If you ever get a group of people into unity for a purpose and you get them into prayer, nothing will be restrained from them if they are in agreement with God. There is awesome power in such agreement.

Gospel Prayer Truths

Here are thirteen gospel prayer truths from Chapter 8:

1. Corporate prayer, with everyone in one accord, can accomplish more than individual prayer.

2. The first step in resolving a conflict is to go alone to the person who is the source of the problem.

3. The second step in resolving a conflict if the first step does not work is to take someone with you to confront the person who is the source of the difficulty (Matthew 18:16).

4. The third step to resolving a conflict if the second step fails is to take your grievance before the proper church officials (Matthew 18:17).

5. Your prayers will be hindered if you don't deal with unresolved conflicts with others.

6. When you come into agreement in prayer with someone, it needs to be more than a mental agreement. It must be a spiritual agreement.

7. If your spirit is clogged up with unforgiveness, bitterness and resentment, your prayers will be hindered.

8. When your ways please the Lord, He will make even your enemies to be at peace with you (Proverbs 16:7).

9. What God has planned for you cannot be stopped by what other people do against you.

10. Reconciliation and restoration are loosed when you forgive someone.

11. Two people in perfect agreement with the Spirit of God make a three-fold cord which is not easily broken (Ecclesiastes 4:12).

12. There is no agreement on the face of the earth more powerful than that of a husband and wife who are in agreement with the Spirit of God.

13. God's plan is for man to take dominion and bring the earth under control for His glory.

QUESTIONS

Part 1. Completion

Please complete each of the statements.

1. When you have been offended by wrongdoing against you, the first step Jesus directs you to take is to go to that person _____ to resolve the situation (Matthew 18: 15).

2. If the first step doesn't work, the second step to resolving a conflict is to take one or two _____ with you to attempt to bring understanding and resolve the conflict (Matthew 18:16). This procedure in the world is called _____.

3. If the first two steps toward reconciliation fail, Jesus gave a third step to take: "And if he refuses to hear them, tell it to the _____ [leadership]. But if he refuses even to hear the church, let him be to you like a _____ and a tax collector" (Matthew 18:17).

4. Proverbs 4:23 admonishes us to keep our hearts with all diligence for out of the heart springs the _____ of life. In other words, we are to protect our spirit man.

5. Proverbs 16:7 says, "When a man's ways please the Lord, He makes even his enemies to be at _____ with him."

6. _____ and _____ are loosed when you forgive, but people are bound when an attitude of _____ prevails.

7. The principle Jesus gave to us in Luke 6:37 is that if we don't judge someone else, we won't be _____; if we don't condemn, we won't be _____; if we forgive, we will be _____.

8. To agree with someone in prayer means there is agreement in the _____.

9. Before you agree with someone in prayer, be sure you are in agreement with God's _____.

10. Ecclesiastes 4:12 says, "A _____ cord is not quickly broken." In other words, the prayer of agreement between a husband and wife who are in perfect agreement with the Spirit of God is a mighty force.

11. Because there was perfect agreement among the people at the tower of Babel, although it was for an evil purpose, God said, "_____ that they propose to do will be withheld from them" (Genesis 11:6). (This is an example of the power of unity, even though God divided their languages to stop the evil.)

Part 2. Personal Application
Please complete the questions and/or statements to the best of your ability.

1. I have resolved a difference (a conflict) with someone successfully by _____

_____

_____

_____

2. I cannot afford to clog my spirit with unforgiveness, bitterness, or resentment because _____

_____

_____

_____

114

CHAPTER 9
UNITED OR CORPORATE PRAYER

T here are several illustrations in the Bible of the effectiveness of united or corporate prayer, both in the Old and New Testaments. Here are a few examples, the principles of which are still relevant for today!

Old Testament Examples
of United or Corporate Prayer

Esther and Her People Saved Through
United Fasting and Prayer

In the book of Esther, a decree was prepared by Haman, an official in the king's court, the intent of which was to destroy the entire Jewish culture. The incident which incited Haman to prepare such a document was that Mordecai, a Jew and the man who had raised Esther after her parents died, would not bow or pay homage to him.

Esther had been placed in a position of authority inside of the palace where she could intervene in this situation and reverse it for her people, although she had to jeopardize her own life to do so. She knew she couldn't even attempt to intervene for her people, the Jews, without united fasting and prayer to uphold her. At her request, Mordecai and the Jewish people came together in united fasting and prayer.

Once Esther learned of the decree, she received Mordecai's admonition:

"Do not think in your heart that you will

escape in the king's palace any more than all the other Jews.

"For if you remain completely silent at this time, relief and deliverance will arise for the Jews from another place, but you and your father's house will perish. Yet who knows whether you have come to the kingdom for such a time as this?"

Esther 4:13,14

Esther's response to Mordecai was:

"Go, gather all the Jews who are present in Shushan, and fast for me; neither eat nor drink for three days, night or day. My maids and I will fast likewise. And so I will go to the king, which is against the law; and if I perish, I perish!"

Esther 4:16

Up until this time, Esther's identity had been hidden. She had been selected to be the queen because of her great beauty, and she had not revealed that she was a Jew.

When wicked Haman got the king to sign a decree certifying that all the Jews would be killed, the king didn't really understand what Haman was doing. Haman was his trusted administrator, and all Haman told him was that there was a group of people who were causing trouble and violating the laws, and he would put up his own money to exterminate them if the king would sign the decree. The king signed it.

Esther became motivated real quick to stand in the gap before the king for her people when she realized she, also a Jew, would not be able to escape death either. Sometimes people have to be motivated with the benefits to gain and the losses to be avoided.

The Jews began to fast and pray for Esther's strategic move to go before the king. There was a law that anyone who went into the inner court of the king without being called would be put to death **"except the one to whom the king holds out the golden scepter, that he may live..."** (Esther 4:11).

As a result of Queen Esther's favor with the king, she invited Haman and the king to two banquets. At the second banquet, she revealed to the king that someone had plotted to kill her and all of her people. Haman was exposed, and he and his sons were hung on the gallows he had prepared for Mordecai while Mordecai was honored. In united fasting and prayer, an entire nation was saved.

The goal of united prayer is to seek the Lord for His help and direction. To "seek the Lord" means to go after Him with all of your heart so His will can be accomplished and His promises attained.

Because Mordecai, Esther and the Jews sought the Lord, their planned extermination was reversed. Letters were prepared and...

> **By these letters the king permitted the Jews who were in every city to gather together and protect their lives—to destroy, kill, and annihilate all the forces of any people or province that would assault them, both little children and women, and to plunder their possessions.**
>
> **Esther 8:11**

Verse 16 says, **"The Jews had light and gladness, joy and honor."** That happened because of united fasting and prayer!

Jehoshaphat and the Israelites Delivered Through United Prayer

A similar situation happened with Jehoshaphat and the Israelites who were surrounded by three enemy armies. Jehoshaphat was a man of God, and he didn't know what to do but pray.

> **It happened after this that the people of Moab with the people of Ammon, and others with them**

besides the Ammonites, came to battle against Jehoshaphat.

Then some came and told Jehoshaphat, saying, "A great multitude is coming against you from beyond the sea, from Syria; and they are in Hazazon Tamar" (which is En Gedi).

And Jehoshaphat feared, and set himself to seek the Lord, and proclaimed a fast throughout all Judah.

So Judah gathered together to ask help from the Lord; and from all the cities of Judah they came to seek the Lord.

Then Jehoshaphat stood in the assembly of Judah and Jerusalem, in the house of the Lord, before the new court,

And said: "O Lord God of our fathers, are You not God in heaven, and do You not rule over all the kingdoms of the nations, and in Your hand is there not power and might, so that no one is able to withstand You?"

2 Chronicles 20:1-6

United prayer doesn't mean that no one prays a singular prayer. As the group was united in seeking the Lord, their prayer was recorded. Evidently there was a time when people stopped and one man expressed the heart cry of the multitude. Wrapped together in one man's prayer, their plight and cry for divine intervention were brought before the Lord.

God doesn't get bothered by everyone praying at once. If He does, He's in big trouble, because there are millions of people all over the world praying at once. He hears individual prayer as well as corporate prayer all at the same time. There are times when one person needs to take the heart cry of what everyone has prayed in corporate prayer and bring it before the Lord.

"Are You not our God, who drove out the inhabitants of this land before Your people Israel, and gave it to the descendants of Abraham Your friend forever?"

2 Chronicles 20:7

Jehoshaphat was putting God in remembrance.

"And they dwell in it, and have built You a sanctuary in it for Your name, saying,

"If disaster comes upon us—sword, judgment, pestilence, or famine—we will stand before this temple and in Your presence (for Your name is in this temple), and cry out to You in our amiction, and You will hear and save."

2 Chronicles 20:8,9

Jehoshaphat was rehearsing the commitment God made to them.

"And now, here are the people of Ammon, Moab, and Mount Seir—whom You would not let Israel invade when they came out of the land of Egypt, but they turned from them and did not destroy them—

"Here they are, rewarding us by coming to throw us out of Your possession which You have given us to inherit."

2 Chronicles 20:10,11

Jehoshaphat's only hope was in God. He knew that without God's help, not only was his neck at stake, but everyone else would be slaughtered, too. He said to God:

"O our God, will You not judge them? For we have no power against this great multitude that is coming against us; nor do we know what to do, but our eyes are upon You."

2 Chronicles 20:12

We have no might or power in our natural ability against the enemy we face in this hour. We have all might and power in the name of Jesus and through the power of the Holy Spirit, but in our natural ability, we don't have the goods to match a former archangel of God who is now bent on destroying the earth and all of its inhabitants. In our natural man, we are no match against the devil. Jehoshaphat said, "Lord, our eyes are on You!" When we get our eyes on the Lord, then we will know what to do.

Jehoshaphat, an anointed king, was rehearsing His condition. He had a covenant with God, but in his own ability, he could do nothing, so he reminded God, "We are no match against this army without Your help, Lord." I think it would be good every day if we remembered that we are dust in our natural ability and that without God, we can't make it.

Jesus rephrased this in the New Testament: **"Without Me you can do nothing"** (John 15:5). Jehoshaphat was saying, "Without You, Lord, we can do nothing. We need Your help."

Jehoshaphat's prayer wasn't a negative prayer. He was simply stating the conditions, rehearsing God's commitment to him and welcoming His help. Let's bring this into the *now*.

How do you pray when you've got three armies coming up against you? Maybe you've got leukemia, tuberculosis and heart problems—three armies coming against you at once. Maybe you have gone through a divorce, you have been abused as a child, or you are without a job.

You have had problems in your past, you have problems in your present and you know there are problems ahead of you in your future. You've got three armies arrayed against you at once with one intent: to annihilate you. Satan and his forces have come to steal, kill and destroy (John 10:10). That's what these armies had come to do. That's why we can take stories from the Old Testament, and they relate to where we are at this very moment in time. They are as up to date as your breath. These things were written as an example for us to learn from.

120

Jehoshaphat and the Israelites cried out to God and fasted, prayed and came into agreement. Jehoshaphat's battle wasn't with flesh and blood, and neither is ours. It was with principalities, powers and rulers of the darkness in heavenly places.

Amos 3:3 says, **"Can two walk together, unless they are agreed?"** Just having a crowd doesn't necessarily produce power nor does it guarantee power. When people are focused on Jesus and they come into agreement, there will be positive results.

God instructed Habakkuk to **"write the vision and make it plain on tablets, that he may run who reads it"** (Habakkuk 2:2).

In united prayer, everyone needs to know why they are praying and the goal toward which they are praying. That means someone has to declare it. Jehoshaphat stood up and declared it.

When people are together but they are praying in different directions, you don't have corporate, united prayer. It's like trying to move a grand piano. It is a lot easier for five people to move it than one. One person simply can't do it, but if five people come at the same time, they can do it.

It is the same way in prayer. If everyone will focus on a singular thing at one time, the united energy will be far greater than the addition of all of our energies going in separate directions.

In other words, if one person tries to lift something, he exerts all of his energy. But if you take the same amount of energy and combine it corporately on a singular object, it will move. That's the power of united prayer. Nothing will be restrained to those who have one mind and are speaking the same thing. Whatever they put their hand to, it will happen.

New Testament Examples
of United or Corporate Prayer

The power of united prayer and the same prayer principles that worked at the tower of Babel, with Esther and with Jehoshaphat, are also found in the New Testament.

121

**The Outpouring of the
Holy Spirit at Pentecost**

In Acts 1, Jesus told the disciples to gather in the upper room and **"wait for the Promise of the Father..."** (Acts 1:4). He was speaking of the baptism with the Holy Spirit.

**"For John truly baptized with water, but you
shall be baptized with the Holy Spirit not many days
from now."**

Acts 1:5

Acts 1:15 indicates that 120 people were gathered in the upper room, which included Mary, the mother of Jesus, the disciples and the brethren of Jesus.

Acts 2:1 speaks of one of the greatest miracles in the Bible.

**When the Day of Pentecost had fully come, they
were all with one accord in one place.**

Can you imagine 120 people in one accord in one place? They were in unity, agreement and harmony.

**And suddenly there came a sound from heaven,
as of a rushing mighty wind, and it filled the whole
house where they were sitting.**

**Then there appeared to them divided tongues,
as of fire, and one sat upon each of them.**

**And they were all filled with the Holy Spirit and
began to speak with other tongues, as the Spirit gave
them utterance.**

Acts 2:2-4

The great events that took place on the day of Pentecost were preceded by people coming into unity. If churches want the power of God today, they must have this same unity. To the degree that people will come into one accord, the Spirit of God will be poured out in like measure.

Peter stood up and said:

"This is what was spoken by the prophet Joel:

"'And it shall come to pass in the last days, says God, that I will pour out of My Spirit on all flesh; your sons and your daughters shall prophesy, your young men shall see visions, your old men shall dream dreams.

"'And on My menservants and on My maid-servants I will pour out My Spirit in those days; and they shall prophesy.'"

Acts 2:16-18

Then Peter said:

"Let all the house of Israel know assuredly that God has made this Jesus, whom you crucified, both Lord and Christ."

Now when they heard this, they were cut to the heart, and said to Peter and the rest of the apostles, "Men and brethren, what shall we do?"

Then Peter said to them, "Repent, and let every one of you be baptized in the name of Jesus Christ for the remission of sins; and you shall receive the gift of the Holy Spirit.

"For the promise is to you and to your children, and to all who are afar off, as many as the Lord our God will call."

Acts 2:36-39

Maybe you have been in places where there was disagreement and disharmony and there was an outpouring, not of the Holy Spirit, but of different spirits—strife, division, fighting and bickering. When we come into agreement, God's Spirit will move. People will be saved and delivered. That's what happened in Acts 2. They were all filled with the Holy Spirit. Then Peter stood up and preached under the anointing of the Holy Spirit and 3,000 people were saved.

We should pray for a fresh outpouring of the Holy Spirit in our lives daily, for the boldness to speak God's Word and for the harvest of souls to be loosed into God's Kingdom.

Lame Man Healed

In Acts 3, Peter and John went down to the temple gate and ministered healing to a lame man. As a result of this man's testimony of healing, 5,000 more people were saved.

Peter and John were headed to the temple together for corporate prayer when this miracle took place. They participated in corporate prayer on a regular basis.

When people pray, not only will people be filled with the Holy Spirit, not only will the Word be spoken with boldness that brings about salvation, but it will also produce an atmosphere for miracles. Corporate prayer will bring the power of God on the scene to meet every need.

Peter spoke to the lame man, **"In the name of Jesus Christ of Nazareth, rise up and walk"** (Acts 3:6).

Verses 7 and 8 indicate the lame man's response:
> **Immediately his feet and ankle bones received strength.**
> **So he, leaping up, stood and walked and entered the temple with them—walking, leaping, and praising God.**

There are four parts to the miracle:
1. Corporate prayer.
2. The lame man's healing.
3. The man's testimony of his healing.
4. Five thousand people were born again.

The Church began with signs, wonders and miracles. There is no reason for us to stop it in this day and hour. If they needed signs, wonders and miracles then, how much more do we need them now? Thank God for medicine and education, but they cannot meet all of the needs of the human race. We need the power of God and the anointing of the Holy Spirit.

As a result of this miracle and the testimony of it, Peter and John ended up before the authorities. They were called in on the carpet, because they had caused a ruckus in Jerusalem by declaring...

> **"And His name** [Jesus' name], **through faith in His name, has made this man strong...Yes, the faith which comes through Him has given him this perfect soundness in the presence of you all."**

> **Acts 3:16**

The high priest rebuked Peter and John and told them not to speak any more in Jesus' name.

> **"Whether it is right in the sight of God to listen to you more than to God, you judge.**
>
> **"For we cannot but speak the things which we have seen and heard."**
>
> **So when they had further threatened them, they let them go, finding no way of punishing them, because of the people, since they all glorified God for what had been done.**
>
> **For the man was over forty years old on whom this miracle of healing had been performed.**
>
> **And being let go, they went to their own companions and reported all that the chief priests and elders had said to them.**
>
> **So when they heard that, they raised their voice to God with one accord and said: "Lord, You are God, who made heaven and earth and the sea, and all that is in them,**
>
> **"Who by the mouth of Your servant David have said: 'Why did the nations rage, and the people plot vain things?**

" 'The kings of the earth took their stand, and
the rulers were gathered together against the Lord
and against His Christ.'
" 'For truly against Your holy Servant Jesus,
whom You anointed, both Herod and Pontius
Pilate, with the Gentiles and the people of Israel,
were gathered together
" 'To do whatever Your hand and Your purpose
determined before to be done.' "

Acts 4:19-28

Peter traces two experiences: one of David and the other of
Jesus. David was faced with all types of obstacles and adverse,
negative circumstances, and he cried out to the Lord, "Why do
the nations rage?" David is the one who said:

The Lord is my shepherd; I shall not want...
Yea, though I walk through the valley of the
shadow of death, I will fear no evil; for You are
with me; Your rod and Your staff, they comfort me.

Psalm 23:1,4

David knew that God would fight for him. Though an army
would encamp round about him, he knew God would be with
him. He declared that in his prayer.

Peter said that all the people were gathered together against
him. He was saying, "I'm in the same position David was in. I'm
in the same position You were in, Jesus." You may be in that position today. The enemy has come, and his plan is the same as it
always has been: to steal, kill and destroy (John 10:10).

Obviously, what Peter and John had done went against the
grain of the kingdom of darkness. It challenged the devil, and
they were persecuted for it.

"Now, Lord, look on their threats, and *grant to*
Your servants that with all boldness they may speak
Your word,

*"By stretching out Your hand to heal, and that
signs and wonders may be done through the name of
Your holy Servant Jesus."*

Acts 4:29,30

This is an hour when we need to pray for holy boldness.
Many have prayed for other people to change or for circumstances in the land to change. Peter didn't pray any of that. He
said, "Lord, let something happen on the inside of us. Grant that
Your servants will be bold."

Peter prayed for the people's lives. He wasn't praying for the
religious leaders who had threatened him, for those who were
going to make laws to intimidate, threaten, or curtail their ministry
activities. He said, "Lord, let Your healing miracles happen."
We need to pray for miracles, signs and wonders—obvious
manifestations of the supernatural—that will give credence and
evidence that Jesus is alive.

Reversing Negative Situations

The prayer of Esther was that she would have favor with the
king so the Jews would be saved. In Jehoshaphat's case, prayer
was for supernatural deliverance in battle. On the day of Pentecost,
they were praying for the promise of the Father. They didn't fully
understand what it was, except He had said the Holy Spirit
would come. They didn't know how He would manifest or what
was going to happen, but they prayed for the outpouring of the
Holy Spirit.

**And when they had prayed, the place where they
were assembled together was shaken; and they were
all filled with the Holy Spirit, and they spoke the
word of God with boldness.**

Acts 4:31

When people come together in one accord in unified prayer,
the whole place will shake with supernatural signs, wonders and
miracles.

127

After the Holy Ghost came on them, they weren't intimidated by the leaders who had threatened them.

> **Now the multitude of those who believed were of one heart and of one soul; neither did anyone say that any of the things he possessed was his own, but they had all things in common.**
>
> **Acts 4:32**

Now we see something else. After they were filled with the Holy Ghost, not only did they speak the Word with boldness, but a spirit of love, unity and compassion for one another came inside of them.

The supernatural manifestations of the power of God should bring us closer together and give us more compassion for one another.

Verse 33 says, **"And with great power the apostles gave witness to the resurrection of the Lord Jesus. And great grace was upon them all."**

Acts 5:12-14 says:

> **And through the hands of the apostles many signs and wonders were done among the people. And they were all with one accord in Solomon's Porch.**
>
> **Yet none of the rest dared join them, but the people esteemed them highly.**
>
> **And believers were increasingly added to the Lord, multitudes of both men and women.**

When there are supernatural signs, wonders and miracles it will result in the salvation of lost people.

> **They brought the sick out into the streets and laid them on beds and couches, that at least the shadow of Peter passing by might fall on some of them.**
>
> **Also a multitude gathered from the surrounding cities to Jerusalem, bringing sick people and**

those who were tormented by unclean spirits, and they were all healed.

Acts 5:15,16

United prayer initiated these miracles. The believers were in agreement in the face of opposition, and God brought the miracles.

When we come into corporate prayer, not only does the Holy Spirit come, not only do miracles happen and people get healed, not only is the Word preached with boldness, resulting in people getting saved, but when we pray in a united way, the Holy Ghost speaks.

We find an example of this in Acts 13:1,2:

Now in the church that was at Antioch there were certain prophets and teachers: Barnabas, Simeon who was called Niger, Lucius of Cyrene, Manaen who had been brought up with Herod the tetrarch, and Saul.

As they ministered to the Lord and fasted, the Holy Spirit said, "Now separate to Me Barnabas and Saul for the work to which I have called them."

United prayer doesn't have to be the church body. It can be a group of people coming into agreement anywhere, praying for God's will to be done.

The family unit is the most powerful unit that can come into agreement in united prayer. No one can get closer than a family who lives together, who are joined together naturally by blood and supernaturally by the blood of Jesus Christ.

Gospel Prayer Truths

Here are thirteen gospel prayer truths from Chapter 9:

1. God has brought *you* to His Kingdom *"for such a time as this"* (Esther 4:14).

2. There is great power in united or corporate fasting and prayer.

3. The goal of united prayer is to seek the Lord for His help and direction.

4. Corporate prayer will reverse negative circumstances.

5. Without God's help, we are no match against the devil in this hour. But resisting the devil with the name of Jesus and the power of the Holy Spirit will cause him to flee from us.

6. As we seek the Lord, He will give us a strategic plan of what to do for every circumstance we face.

7. Our battle is not with flesh and blood, but with principalities, powers and rulers of the darkness.

8. Prayer within a group of people who are praying in different directions does not constitute corporate or united prayer. There must be a designated prayer goal for which everyone is praying for it to be corporate or united prayer.

9. To the degree that people will come into one accord, the Spirit will be poured out in like measure.

10. You can pray for a fresh outpouring of the Holy Spirit in your life each day.

11. Corporate or united prayer creates an atmosphere that is conducive to signs, wonders and miracles.

12. Corporate prayer sets the stage for the Holy Spirit to speak.

13. The corporate prayer of a family unit is one of the strongest sources of effective prayer.

QUESTIONS

Part 1. Completion

Please complete each of the statements.

1. When Esther was faced with the task of intervening before the king for the Jews because of a decree Haman had published to destroy the Jews, Mordecai said to her, "Yet who knows whether you have come to the kingdom for _____ _____ _____ _____ _____ ?" (Esther 4:14).

2. Because her own life was in jeopardy to go before the king when she had not been called, Esther called the Jews to a three-day fast with her. She said, "And so I will go to the king,which is against the law; and if I perish, _____ _____ !" (Esther 4:16).

3. The goal of united prayer is to seek the Lord for His _____ and _____ .

4. When Jehoshaphat and the Israelites were surrounded by three enemy armies, Scripture says Jehoshaphat "set himself to _____the Lord, and proclaimed a _____ throughout all Judah" (2 Chronicles 20:3).

5. In 2 Chronicles 20:12, Jehoshaphat prayed, "For we have no power against this great multitude that is coming against us; nor do we know what to do, but our eyes are upon _____ ."

6. Jesus said, "Without Me you can do _____ " (John 15:5).

7. What three things did Jehoshaphat and the Israelites do in strategizing to get God's plan for their situation?

    a. _____

    b. _____

    c. _____

8. Our battles, just as Jehoshaphat's, are not with flesh and blood, but with:

   a. _____

   b. _____

   c. _____

9. In united prayer, those involved need to know:

   a. _____

   b. _____

10. The "promise of the Father" Jesus spoke of in Acts 1:4 is the _____ with the Holy Spirit.

11. On the Day of Pentecost, 120 people were "with _____ accord in _____ place" (Acts 2:1).

12. As a result of Peter's message on the Day of Pentecost, 3,000 people were added to the Church. Peter said:

    "Repent, and let every one of you be baptized in the name of Jesus Christ for the _____ _____ _____; and you shall receive the _____ of the Holy Spirit. "For the promise is to you and to your children, and to all who are afar off, as many as the Lord our God will call" (Acts 2:38,39).

13. The four parts to the lame man's miracle in Acts 3 are:

    a. _____

    b. _____

    c. _____

    d. _____

14. Peter and John declared that the power source for the lame man's healing was faith in the name of _____ (Acts 3: 16).

15. When people come together in unified prayer, supernatural

_____, _____and

_____ result.

16. The most powerful unit that can come together in agreement in united prayer is the _____ unit.

Part 2. Personal Application

Please complete the questions and/or statements to the best of your ability.

1. My battle strategy against the enemy includes _____

_____

_____

_____

_____

_____

2. The power source of miracles in my life and in the lives of those for whom I am praying is _____

_____

_____

3. To be in one accord in prayer agreement will result in

_____

_____

_____

_____

CHAPTER 10

THE EPHESIANS PRAYERS

Praying the Word of God is the most effective way to pray, because to pray the Word is to pray the will of God. God's ways and thoughts are rained down upon us from heaven by the Word of God. That's the analogy Isaiah draws in Isaiah 55:10 and 11. Just as the rain and snow come from the atmosphere above us and they produce on the earth, in the same way, God's Word rains down His thoughts, ideas and ways into the earth so we can know them.

It's one thing to say, "His ways and thoughts are above us," but we need to complete this passage of scripture: "God has brought His ways, His ideas and thoughts into the earth by the seed of His Word." We can know God's ways, ideas and thoughts by reading His Word.

We know from what Jesus said in Mark 4:14-20 that if we will *hear the Word, believe it* and *receive it*, we will be good ground and will be blessed in the earth.

"The sower sows the word.

"And these are the ones by the wayside where the word is sown. When they hear, Satan comes immediately and takes away the word that was sown in their hearts.

"These likewise are the ones sown on stony ground who, when they hear the word, immediately receive it with gladness;

"And they have no root in themselves, and so

**endure only for a time. Afterward, when tribula-
tion or persecution arises for the word's sake,
immediately they stumble.**

**"Now these are the ones sown among thorns;
they are the ones who hear the word,**

**"And the cares of this world, the deceitfulness
of riches, and the desires for other things entering
in choke the word, and it becomes unfruitful.**

**"But these are the ones sown on good ground,
those who hear the word, accept it, and bear fruit:
some thirtyfold, some sixty, and some a hundred."**

God sends forth His Word, and those who believe it and lay
hold of it will be good ground. We will bring forth fruit in our
lives by obedience to God's Word.

Through God's Word, we begin to understand God's ways
and thoughts. It's the same way in prayer. Many people have
asked, "What should I pray? How can I pray more effectively?
How can I pray something that will get results?" *If you pray
God's Word, you will get results*, because His Word reveals His
will, plans and purposes.

The best thing to do is find out what God is doing and do it.
Then you won't even have to pray that it be blessed, because God
automatically blesses what He initiates. That's like someone
praying for their finances to be blessed. If they aren't a tither, they
have negated the channel through which God plans to bless them.

The Ephesians 1 Prayer

Paul gave a prayer in Ephesians 1 and another in Ephesians 3
that every believer should pray every day. First, let's look at
Paul's prayer in Ephesians 1:15-23:

**Therefore I also, after I heard of your faith in
the Lord Jesus and your love for all the saints,**

**Do not cease to give thanks for you, making
mention of you in my prayers:**

That the God of our Lord Jesus Christ, the Father of glory, may give to you the spirit of wisdom and revelation in the knowledge of Him,

The eyes of your understanding being enlightened; that you may know what is the hope of His calling, what are the riches of the glory of His inheritance in the saints,

And what is the exceeding greatness of His power toward us who believe, according to the working of His mighty power

Which He worked in Christ when He raised Him from the dead and seated Him at His right hand in the heavenly places,

Far above all principality and power and might and dominion, and every name that is named, not only in this age but also in that which is to come.

And He put all things under His feet, and gave Him to be the head over all things to the church,

Which is His body, the fullness of Him who fills all in all.

Paul was saying, "I am praying that your inner man would become stronger and that you would be much bigger on the inside than you are on the outside, that you would be flooded with revelation knowledge and light and that Christ would stand up in you so when people see you, they see Jesus. When you touch someone then Jesus has touched them."

Your Ephesians 1 prayer could go something like this:

Thank You, Father, that because I am in Christ Jesus as a born-again believer, You have given me a spirit of wisdom and revelation in the knowledge of You.

The eyes of my understanding are being enlightened that I may know the hope of Your calling in my life and the riches of the

glory of Your inheritance for me. Thank You, Father, for enlightening my understanding to the exceeding greatness of Your power toward me, according to the working of Your mighty power, which You worked in Christ when You raised Him from the dead and seated Him at Your right hand in heavenly places, far above all principality and power and might and dominion and every name that is named, in this age as well as in that which is to come.

Thank You, Father, that You put all things under Jesus' feet and made Him to be the head over all things to the Church, which is Your Body.

Holy Spirit, reveal Jesus Christ in me. Bring to my remembrance everything Jesus said. Strengthen me in my inner man, that there would be no weakness on the inside of me, no character flaws, no place for the enemy, no depression, no discouragement, no fear; no doubt, no lust, no anger; but that love, faith, joy and peace would rule in my inner man in the name of Jesus Christ of Nazareth.

I encourage you to pray this prayer every day.

The "spirit of wisdom" means an ongoing unveiling or a continual revelation. The Holy Spirit will give to you the spirit of wisdom and knowledge in the revelation of Jesus Christ, that Jesus will become unveiled to you.

Ephesians 1:3 says we have already been blessed **"with every spiritual blessing in the heavenly places in Christ."** In other words, everything we will ever need pertaining to this life and the life to come has already been provided through Jesus Christ.

In the fall of Adam and Eve, man lost the position, righteousness, eternal life and authority he once had, but in the crucifixion and resurrection of Jesus Christ, He regained what was lost. He redeemed us, so from a natural standpoint in creation and from a supernatural standpoint in the spiritual realm, through the resurrection, everything we need naturally and spiritually has already been provided for us in Jesus Christ.

No wonder Paul asked the Father to give us **"the spirit of wisdom and revelation in the knowledge of Him,"** (Ephesians 1:17) because **"in Him we live and move and have our being..."** (Acts 17:28). In Christ we have the fullness of life.

Paul's cry was that we would understand Jesus Christ, and it should be our heart's cry that we become like Jesus.

Jesus was already crucified, resurrected and ascended to the Father, and He had sent the Holy Spirit. Paul was praying that our hearts would be flooded with light.

Many people are "in the dark" in their relationship with Jesus Christ. They may have heard about Him, but to them He is a stained-glass Jesus or a historical Jesus. Many people can quote historical facts, but they don't have a revelation of what Christ did as it relates to their lives.

I grew up reading the Bible, but there was a day when someone explained salvation to me. Then I understood what it meant to be saved and how to be saved.

I remember when I began to understand that God's Word is true, but every man is a liar (Romans 3:4). I began to understand that you could believe the truth of God's Word and speak it over natural facts and circumstances that were contrary to the Word, and if you stood by the Word, God would change the natural circumstances.

Until the Word becomes revelation to your inner man, as opposed to head knowledge, you won't be changed. This is why Paul prayed that the eyes of our understanding would be enlightened.

To know " the hope of your calling" is to know that you have been called into the family of the Lord Jesus Christ, and you have been called into eternity to live with God the Father in heaven.

Every person who hears the voice of Jesus Christ and responds to it will hear that calling.

Paul prayed that we would understand "the riches of the glory of God's inheritance" in us. An inheritance is that which someone is given legally from someone who dies. Jesus' death took place at Calvary. Jesus not only died, releasing the inheritance to us, but He arose from the dead. That means He is now the Advocate, the Lawyer, or the Trustee Who will insure that the inheritance gets to the rightful heirs.

Wouldn't it be wonderful in all inheritance cases if the one who died could come back and make sure everyone received what was coming to them? In the natural, the big arguments come in when people can't figure out the intent and purpose of the person who made out the will.

Jesus rose from the dead to make sure we know our inheritance. He sent the Holy Spirit as the earnest deposit of His inheritance to us. Through all eternity, God will continue to unveil the riches of Jesus Christ, for we have only begun to understand the glorious, marvelous redemption that is in Christ.

We have inherited Jesus' name, and we have inherited His life. It's no small thing to have the zoe life of God flowing in our veins! It's no small thing to have the Holy Spirit dwelling inside of us.

Every promise in the Bible is a part of our inheritance, and all that we walk upon by faith we will have in our lives.

Paul also prayed that we would understand the exceeding greatness of God's power toward us who believe. Paul was saying, "I want you to know how much power has been made available to you. This power is according to the working of His mighty power."

The two aspects of this power are:

1. *Authority*, like a policeman directing traffic has authority because a chief, a mayor and a city system have invested authority in him, with a badge and a uniform signifying that authority.

140

He can stand up in the middle of a road, hold up his hand and cars have to stop. That is authority because of position.

2. *Dunamis* is explosive power, ability and might. It is one thing to have the authority, but it is another thing to have the awesome power inside of us to speak and see sicknesses and diseases removed.

The power Paul was talking about is the same power that God used to raise Jesus from the dead. Some people pray, "God, give me power to resist the devil." Paul is saying, "When you were born again, the same Spirit that raised Christ from the dead was put inside of you." If you knew the power that was on the inside of you, you wouldn't complain about depression, discouragement, or "the devil did this or that."

Some people get bugged with me, because through the years, I have not talked a great deal about negative things or about the things the devil has done. They say, "Come on, be real. There's got to be things going wrong." My response is, "God is doing great things in our lives. Heaven has broken loose upon us. The enemy flees from us."

James says if you humble yourself and submit to God, you can expect the devil to flee. Why say anything else when you have the resurrection power of God working inside of you? To say anything else is to contradict the revelation of Jesus on the inside of you.

I'm not saying that we don't have to resist the enemy, for James 4:7 says, **"Therefore *submit* to God. *Resist* the devil and he will flee from you."**

If no resistance was needed, James wouldn't have mentioned it. Paul wouldn't have mentioned resisting the fiery darts of the enemy with the shield of faith and the sword of the Spirit if no resistance to the devil was needed (Ephesians 6:16,17). Peter wouldn't have mentioned the need to be sober and vigilant because the devil walks about as a roaring lion seeking whom he may devour if no resistance to the adversary, Satan, was needed (1 Peter 5:8).

Each of these men talk about the devil from the aspect that he has already been defeated and conquered, which he has and which is the view we are to take, but they do say that we must *resist the devil.*

Paul continues the Ephesians 1 prayer, **"And He** [God the Father] **put all things under His** [Jesus'] **feet, and gave Him to be head over all things to the church, which is His body..."** (vv. 22,23). If Jesus has had all things put under His feet and you are part of the Body of Christ, then the principalities and powers of the devil *are under your feet!*

The bottom line is, "Did Jesus do enough? Did His blood pay for all of your sins? Did He really defeat the devil, or is that yet to happen?" Colossians 2:15 says Jesus disarmed the devil of his authority, power, might and dominion. When Jesus was raised from the dead, He said, **"I am he that liveth, and was dead; and, behold, I am alive for evermore, Amen; and have the keys of hell and of death"** (Revelation 1:18 KJV).

In Matthew 28:18,19, Jesus said:

> **"All authority has been given to Me in heaven and on earth.**
>
> **"Go therefore and make disciples of all the nations, baptizing them in the name of the Father and of the Son and of the Holy Spirit."**

If Jesus has *all* authority and you are in His Body—the Body of Christ—then Paul was saying, "I am praying that you will get a revelation of what Jesus has already done for you." We aren't going *to* a victory, but we are proceeding *from* a victory! It has already been won. We are walking out a victory that has already been accomplished! We are enforcing Satan's defeat, which has already been accomplished. That's why we must keep our words in line with God's Word.

At the heart of Paul's prayer, he was saying, "I pray that you really know Jesus, not with denominational eyeglasses, not with traditions of men, not with the elements of the world, but that you would know Him as the resurrected King!"

The Ephesians 3 Prayer

Victory in life is absolute if we appropriate the provision Jesus has already made for us.

Effective prayer is simply agreeing with God. If you find out what God's will is in His Word and you agree with it and ask for it to be done, you can be assured God will release the power to bring it to pass, because He initiated it. *His plans are blessed.*

The Ephesians 3 prayer is found in verses 14-19.

For this reason I bow my knees to the Father of our Lord Jesus Christ,

From whom the whole family in heaven and earth is named.

Verses 14,15

Who has the family name? Jesus has the family name, and the whole family of God in heaven and earth has been named after Him. The word *Christian* means "little Christ." If you call yourself a Christian, you are calling yourself "one like Jesus Christ," because you have His life and nature in you and you are following Him.

We are part of a worldwide Body, or family, in heaven and in earth. The believers who have already died are just as real, alive, active, and a whole lot more alert and turned on than we are, because they see Jesus face to face. That's why grieving over a loved one who has gone on to glory is only a temporary thing for a believer. We're not to sorrow as the world sorrows, because we have a promise of resurrection.

That doesn't mean you won't miss a person, but it's the same as if someone says, "I am moving to Arizona." You may cry a tear

143

over their leaving, but you know you will see them again. You will see loved ones again who have gone to heaven, because we are part of the same family.

Paul continues:

That He would grant you, according to the riches of His glory, to be strengthened with might through His Spirit in the inner man.

Ephesians 3:16

The inner man of people who are born again but who don't feed on the Word, don't pray and don't obey the Word, is very weak. They know Christ and they know what to do and how to do it, but they are incapable of doing it because their inner man is so weak.

Jesus said in John 3:7, **"You must be born again."** When you are born again, like a newborn baby in the natural, you aren't born fully mature. You are born as a baby. Peter said, **"As newborn babes, desire the pure milk of the word, that you may grow thereby"** (1 Peter 2:2). *The King James Version* calls it, **"the sincere milk of the word...."**

Jesus said, **"Man shall not live by bread alone, but by every word that proceeds from the mouth of God"** (Matthew 4:4).

The writer of Hebrews talked about milk and solid food or strong meat in the believer's life:

For everyone who partakes only of milk is unskilled in the word of righteousness, for he is a babe.

But solid food belongs to those who are of full age, that is, those who by reason of use have their senses exercised to discern both good and evil.

Hebrews 5:13,14

Jesus said to His disciples when they encouraged Him to eat after His confrontation with the woman at the well:

144

**"I have food to eat of which you do not know ...
"My food is to do the will of Him who sent
Me, and to finish His work."**

John 4:32,34

"Strong meat," as *The King James Version* says, is to do
the will of God. Many people think strong meat is some strange
revelation that only a few sophisticated intellectuals can comprehend. "Strong meat" isn't sitting around listening to some new
revelation. It is to do God's will as Jesus said. Jesus was a soulwinner. He led the woman at the well who was drawing natural
water to a place where she could receive living water! Being a
soulwinner is "strong meat." Paul prayed that we would **"be
strengthened with might through His** [God's] **Spirit in the
inner man"** (Ephesians 3:16).

We are strengthened in the inner man by the milk, the bread
and the meat of God's Word. We are also strengthened by praying
in the Holy Spirit. **"But you, beloved, building yourselves up on
your most holy faith, praying in the Holy Spirit"** (Jude 20).

Paul said in 1 Corinthians 14:4, **"He who speaks in a tongue
edifies himself...."** To *edify* means "to build up or strengthen."

We are strengthened by doing what is right. An inner character development takes place when we do what is right, while the
inner man of people who do what is wrong and violate their
conscience is weakened.

Love strengthens a person. People who are cruel, unmerciful
and unforgiving have a weak inner man, because where envy and
strife exist, there is confusion and every evil work (James 3:16).
When you walk in love and refuse strife, bitterness, resentment
and unforgiveness, your inner man will be strengthened.

Paul was saying, "I pray that you will be strengthened in your
inner man so that you will refuse evil and be strong enough to
help someone else." The strong are to bear the burdens of the
weak (Romans 15:1). Some people say they have arrived at a cer-

tain place where all of their needs are met. They are blessed, happy and going through life not realizing that when they reach a point where they are blessed, they have an obligation to bless someone else. When we are strong, we have an obligation to strengthen others.

We are to become givers, not takers, and set a priority in our lives, "I am going to be a giver. I will be a stream, a conduit, a vehicle, a vessel for the glory, power, goodness and graciousness of God to flow through."

When you have to stretch your faith, your inner man is strengthened. We, as a Body at Victory Christian Center, are stretching our faith and believing for buildings, missionaries and ordained ventures into other parts of the world. In the natural, when you stretch your muscles with weights and you continue to increase the weights, your muscles will become stronger.

The reward of faithfulness is more responsibility. As you are given more responsibility, your faith muscles and your inner man will be renewed and strengthened.

One man said, "I'm a thousand times bigger on the inside than I am on the outside." Don't ever judge a person by their outward appearance! A little child can have his inner man so strong in the Word that his prayers are answered immediately. A frail little lady of 85 pounds who knows how to pray and intercede can bring heaven and earth together. Some people who are big hulks on the outside are shriveled up on the inside with no love, joy, or peace.

When you consider someone for marriage, judge the inward person. Are they people of character? Is their spirit strong? Are they full of love, faith and power? When prayer is needed, do they go get someone else, or are they ready to pray? When it comes time to worship, do they have their hands in their pockets counting squares on the ceiling? The person who is strong in his or her spirit is a strong worshipper.

Your inward man will affect your outer countenance.

Proverbs 18:14 says, **"Who can bear a broken spirit?"** The strength of a man's spirit will sustain him in an attack. If you are strong on the inside, it doesn't matter what comes on the outside. You can stand up against it. That's why you should feed your inner man. Some people feed their outer man but starve their inner man. You ought to fast the outer man and overload the inner man with the Word of God! Take an overdose of the Word!

Luke 21:34 KJV says:

> **And take heed to yourselves, lest at any time your hearts be overcharged with surfeiting, and drunkenness, and cares of this life, and so that day come upon you unawares.**

Surfeiting means "overindulgence or excess, particularly in relationship to food and drink." Their stomach has become their god. To bring the body under control, the inner man needs to be strengthened and the mind renewed.

Second Corinthians 10:5 KJV says we can bring our thoughts under control.

> **Casting down imaginations and every high thing that exalteth itself against the knowledge of God, and bringing into captivity every thought to the obedience of Christ.**

It's an effort to build your inner man strong enough where you listen to the voice on the inside instead of the voice on the outside. The flesh will always try to go the opposite direction of your spirit, but if your mind is renewed with the Word of God, you will tell your body what it is going to do.

Fasting is good for you, not only so you can hear the voice of the Holy Spirit more clearly, but because it is a time where you say, "Body, you are not going to eat." The body says, "I am, too. You're not going to starve me." But you say, "No, body, you are under the subjection of the Holy Spirit. You are under subjection to the Word of God, and I am putting you under my spirit and under my mind. I have a born-again spirit, a renewed mind and a submitted body."

Many people struggle to walk in victory, because their spirit man is not strong. When you continually hear, study and meditate upon the Word, you've got a tiger in your tank as far as your spirit man being built up and strengthened! Instead of a weak kitten purring, a roar is coming, because the Lion of the Tribe of Judah is standing up on the inside of you!!

The Holy Spirit says, "I pray that Christ would dwell in your hearts by faith, that you would be rooted and grounded in love, that you would be able to comprehend the width and length and depth and height of Christ's love and that you may be filled with all the knowledge of God."

When you are strong on the inside, you can walk in love and forgiveness. People who can't forgive an offense that has been done to them are not strong enough in their inner man. A person who is strong on the inside is quick to say, "I forgive you" when an offense comes.

Your spirit can become so strong that you, like Stephen, will cry out to the Father when an offense comes, **"Lord, do not charge them with this sin"** (Acts 7:60).

Pray Ephesians 3 on a daily basis for others as well as for yourself. Your Ephesians 3 prayer could go something like this:

I bow my knees to the Father of the Lord Jesus Christ, from whom the whole family in heaven and earth is named.

Thank You, Father, for granting me, according to the riches of Your glory, to be strengthened with might through Your Spirit in my inner man.

Lord Jesus, You dwell in my heart through faith. Being rooted and grounded in love, I am able to comprehend the width and length and depth and height of the Father's love, so l may be filled with His fullness.

148

Gospel Prayer Truths

Here are fifteen gospel prayer truths from Chapter 10:

1. To pray God's Word is to pray His will.
2. We can know God's ways, ideas and thoughts by reading His Word.
3. Your life will bear fruit for God's Kingdom as you are obedient to His Word.
4. You can pray the Ephesians 1 prayer each day, thanking God for the spirit of wisdom and revelation in the knowledge of Him, and that the eyes of your understanding are enlightened.
5. If you will put agreement with God's Word, He will change your natural circumstances to line up with His Word.
6. Every promise in the Bible is part of the inheritance of the born-again believer.
7. We are walking out a victory that already has been won. We enforce Satan's defeat with our own words.
8. Effective prayer is simply agreeing with God.
9. Part of the Ephesians 3 prayer is to pray to be strengthened with might through the Holy Spirit in your inner man.
10. To feed on God's Word, pray and obey the Word, will strengthen your inner man.
11. "Strong meat" is to do the will of God, just as Jesus did.
12. To speak in tongues is to edify or build yourself up (1 Corinthians 14:4).
13. The strength in your inward man will affect your outer countenance.
14. The strength of your spirit man will sustain you in the time of attack.
15. If you are strong in your inner man through prayer, you will be able to cast down imaginations and thoughts that do not agree with God's Word (2 Corinthians 10:5).

149

QUESTIONS

Part 1. Completion

Please complete each of the statements.

1. God's Word rains down His _____ _____ and _____ into the earth.

2. If we _____ the Word, _____ it and _____ it, we will be blessed in the earth.

3. According to Mark 4:19, what three things choke the Word out of a person, causing it to be unfruitful?

   a. _____

   b. _____

   c. _____

4. In Ephesians 1:17-19, Paul prayed that God would give us the spirit of _____ and _____ in the knowledge of Him, that the eyes of our _____ would be enlightened, that we would know the hope of God's _____ upon our lives, the riches of the glory of His _____ and the exceeding greatness of His _____ toward us who believe.

5. God put all things under _____ feet and gave Him to be the Head over all things to the Church (Ephesians 1:22).

6. James said if we are _____ to God, then we can resist the devil and he will flee (James 4:7).

7. We are to resist the fiery darts of the devil with the shield of _____ and the sword of the Spirit, which is the _____ of God (Ephesians 6:16,17).

8. When Jesus was resurrected, He had with Him the keys of _____ and _____ (Revelation 1:18).

9. Victory in life is absolute if we appropriate the _____ Jesus already made for us.

150

10. We will grow up spiritually by consistently feeding upon God's _____ (Matthew 4:4; 1 Peter 2:2).

11. In addition to being strengthened in the inner man through God's Word, we are strengthened by "praying in the _____ _____" (Jude 20).

12. In 1 Corinthians 14:4, Paul said to speak in tongues is to _____ yourself.

13. A person who is strong in the inside is quick to _____ when an offense comes.

14. When Stephen was faced with an undeserved offense, he said, "Lord, do not _____ them with this sin" (Acts 7:60).

Part 2. Personal Application

Please complete the questions and/or statements to the best of your ability.

1. The Ephesians prayers are important for my own life because

_____

_____

_____

_____

_____

2. My inheritance in Christ is _____

_____

_____

_____

_____

3. The hope of God's calling upon my life is _____

    _____

    _____

    _____

    _____

4. In Christ, I have been given authority to _____

    _____

    _____

    _____

    _____

5. I am becoming stronger in my spirit man by _____

    _____

    _____

    _____

    _____

    _____

CHAPTER 11
THE PRAYER OF COMMITMENT

Casting all your care upon Him, for He cares for you.

1 Peter 5:7

To cast your care on the Lord is to roll your burdens, worries, anxieties and heaviness over on Him. When you do that, you will have freedom, peace, liberty and joy instead of cares and worries.

The prayer of commitment involves the commitment of your entire being to God.

Psalm 37:5 ties in with 1 Peter 5:7:

Commit your way to the Lord, trust also in Him, and He shall bring it to pass.

We are to cast our cares upon the Lord, commit our way to Him, trust in Him and He will bring His will and purposes to pass. In other words, "I surrender my will to God's will." This is what the prayer of commitment is all about. "I am casting the whole of my care over upon the Lord, because He cares for me. I am committing my way unto Him, because He directs my path. He will guide me. He will cause all things to work together for my good because I love Him and I am called according to His purpose."

When cares try to come back on you, you can say, "Oh no, I have cast that care upon the Lord." People carry many burdens God never intended for them to carry—worries, fears and anxieties.

When you cast your care on the Lord, that doesn't mean you don't do anything. You follow the leading of the Holy Spirit, but not out of fear. Some people do their casting on the Lord like a fisherman. They cast it out and then reel it back in!

Proverbs 16:3 says:

Commit your works to the Lord, and your thoughts will be established.

The Amplified Translation of this verse says:

Roll your works upon the Lord [commit and trust them wholly to Him; He will cause your thoughts to become agreeable to His will, and] so shall your plans be established and succeed.

As you commit your works to the Lord, your thoughts will come in line with the will of God. Commit your works—your job, relationships, marriage, attitudes and desires—totally upon the Lord.

Proverbs 3:5,6 says:

Trust in the Lord with all your heart, and lean not on your own understanding;

In all your ways acknowledge Him, and He shall direct your paths.

We are talking about the prayer of commitment. I am committing all of my ways to Him. "Lord, I acknowledge You as Lord of my life. I acknowledge that You have the right to direct and control me in what I am to do. Is this the job for me? Is this the place I am to move?"

In the purchase of a car, an appliance, a dress, a suit, whatever it is, commit it to the Lord. God will become involved in those areas you commit to Him. I believe many people commit certain things to the Lord, but then they go on their own in other areas. We are to continually allow the Lord to be in our thoughts and acknowledge Him every day.

Matthew 6:10 contains the real catalyst of the prayer of commitment. It's where Jesus taught His disciples to pray, **"Your kingdom come. Your will be done on earth as it is in heaven"** (Matthew 6:10). That's a prayer of commitment. It is committing your life to the rulership of the Kingdom of God—that Jesus is the King, and you want Him to direct and lead you in everything you do. You can pray, "Lord, Your Kingdom come in my life."

We know the Kingdom of God is righteousness, peace and joy in the Holy Ghost (Romans 14:17). The Kingdom is where King Jesus rules, so it means you are saying, "Jesus, I want You to rule in my life." The Kingdom of God is not an abstract thing. It isn't some mist in the clouds, an idea, or a thought. Very simply, *the Kingdom is where the King rules.*

The Holy Spirit is the One Who administrates God's Kingdom in the earth under the authority of the King, the lordship of Jesus Christ, as He rules and reigns in our lives.

In heaven, Jesus rules the entire Kingdom of God. In the earth, there are lots of people and places where Jesus is not ruling as King. I have heard people say, "Everything that happens in this world is under God's control." In the earth right now, evil things are happening that are not the will of God. Jesus would not have told us to pray, "Thy kingdom come, thy will be done," if it was already being done. If it happened regardless of our prayers, why would He instruct us to pray it? There is no reason for this to be taught to the disciples or to us if things happen automatically.

Let's do a little backtracking to better understand what I am saying. God gave Adam and Eve dominion and authority in the earth. Adam and Eve surrendered that authority to Satan when they disobeyed God. Satan then became the prince or god of this world. That doesn't mean God couldn't intervene.

God got Noah's attention and saved a righteous family. He got Abraham's attention, who left one land to go to another and establish a great nation. He got Mary's attention to believe and receive the power to conceive His Son, Jesus Christ. He got Paul's attention on the road to Damascus. In each of these cases, in the middle of darkness, God got people's attention to bring Jesus Christ into the earth.

Jesus Christ defeated Satan, took his authority from him, and then said to us:

Behold, I give you the authority to trample on serpents and scorpions, and over all the power of the enemy, and nothing shall by any means hurt you.

Luke 10:19

If you don't know you have power in the name of Jesus, then you are still under the lying authority of the devil. I say "lying authority" because the only authority the devil has is where he has deceived someone. If people don't know the name of Jesus and don't know the truth, they are still under Satan's rulership. Jesus defeated Satan and set us free. Under Satan's rulership, we're like people in a prisoner of war camp. The human race is in the P.O.W. camp of planet earth. Jesus came and broke the chains and liberated us. He announced deliverance to the captives, but some people are still in the P.O.W. camp.

Jesus said:

"If you abide in My word, you are My disciples indeed.

"And you shall know the truth, and the truth shall make you free."

John 8:31,32

The more we study and meditate on the Word of God, the more we can see that Jesus set us free from Satan's works. We must take the Word and declare over our lives, "Lord, Your will be done, Your Kingdom come in me." Why? Because to this point, Satan has not been bound and cast into the lake of fire. Peter said, **"Be sober, be vigilant; because your adversary the devil walks about like a roaring lion, seeking whom he may devour"** (1 Peter 5:8).

That means there are people who are being devoured, who have been devoured, or who will yet be devoured. Only people with an ostrich mentality believe the devil is not real. You don't have to look very far to see that the enemy has affected millions of lives.

God gives us power through the name of Jesus, through the new birth, through the indwelling presence of the Holy Spirit and through His Word to commit ourselves totally to His will.

In the Garden of Gethsemane, Jesus had two different choices. One was a human choice: **"O My Father, if it is possible, let this cup pass from Me..."** (Matthew 26:39). The second choice was a prayer of commitment: **"Nevertheless, not as I will, but as You will"** (v. 39).

Jesus' suffering was more than just the human martyrdom that other people have gone through for a great cause. He took the sins and the punishment of the whole world upon Himself. We have no comprehension of the horror of it, except that Jesus sweat drops of blood facing that decision. Knowing the horrible cup of suffering He would drink, Jesus still committed Himself totally to the will of the Father.

There is a place for each of us to pray a prayer of commitment. Sometimes this particular prayer is neglected in a faith-believing, faith-teaching group.

There are times when you can take God's promises, believe them, speak them, stand upon them and declare them in a specific area that is revealed and known, but there are other areas where you don't know what to do where you will have to commit your way to God.

In the selection of a marriage partner, you can't just claim a certain person. Instead, pray a prayer of commitment for God's will to be done. Some people are naming and claiming certain things when they need to be praying, "Lord, Your will be done." Once God's will is revealed, then you can commit yourself to it.

Once you commit something to the Lord, praise and thank Him for the answer. God can answer the prayer of commitment just as quickly as He can answer the prayer of faith. When you say, "Lord, I don't know exactly what to do, but my eyes are on You," God can bring the answer very quickly. I have seen it happen time and time again when we have committed something to the Lord. He brings the answer supernaturally when we surrender everything to Him!

Gospel Prayer Truths

Here are ten gospel prayer truths from Chapter 11:

1. The prayer of commitment involves the commitment of your entire being to God.

2. Once you cast your cares upon the Lord, commit your way to Him and trust in Him, He will bring His will and purpose to pass in your life.

3. As you commit your works to the Lord, your thoughts will come in line with His will.

4. As you acknowledge God in all of your ways, He will direct your paths (Proverbs 3:6).

5. God will become involved in the areas you commit to Him.

6. The heart of the prayer of commitment is, "Father, Your Kingdom come and Your will be done on earth and in me as it is in heaven" (Matthew 6:10).

7. The Holy Spirit is the One Who administrates God's Kingdom in the earth under the authority of King Jesus.

8. Circumstances don't change automatically. They change because of prayer.

9. Because of Jesus' completed work at Calvary, He has given us authority over all the power of the enemy (Luke 10:19).

10. God will bring answers to your prayers supernaturally when you surrender everything to Him.

QUESTIONS

Part 1. Completion

Please complete each of the statements.

1.   Because God cares for you, Peter said you should cast _____ of your care upon Him (1 Peter 5:7).

2.   The prayer of commitment involves a _____ surrender of your life to God.

3.   Proverbs 16:3 says that as you commit your works to the Lord, your _____ will be established. *The Amplified Translation* of this verse says, "Roll your works upon the Lord [commit and trust them wholly to Him; He will cause your thoughts to become agreeable to His will, and] so shall your plans be _____ and _____."

4.   Proverbs 3:5,6 says that God will _____ the paths of the person who fully trusts in the Lord and acknowledges Him in all of his or her ways.

5.   The prayer of commitment is surrendering your life to the _____ of the Kingdom of God.

6.   The _____ is the One Who administrates God's Kingdom in the earth under the authority of King Jesus.

7.   When Jesus Christ defeated Satan at Calvary, He took Satan's authority and said to you and me as believers in Him, "Behold, I give you the _____ to trample on serpents and scorpions, and over _____ the power of the enemy, and _____ shall by any means hurt you" (Luke 10:19).

8.   Jesus said we would know the truth and the truth would make us free if we _____ in Him (John 8:31,32).

159

9. A perfect example of "total commitment" is Jesus in the Garden of Gethsemane as He prayed to the Father, "Not as I will, but as _____ will" (Matthew 26:39).

Part 2. Personal Application

Please complete the questions and/or statements to the best of your ability.

1. Because I now understand the importance of a full commitment to Christ, I am _____

    _____

    _____

    _____

    _____

2. I am trusting in the Lord in these areas of my life:

    _____

    _____

    _____

    _____

3. I am reigning in this life because of _____

    _____

    _____

    _____

    _____

    _____

160

CHAPTER 12

PRAYING IN THE SPIRIT

When I first heard about the Holy Ghost and later about praying in the Spirit, my only reference to "ghost" was the cartoon character, Casper. I had no comprehension of what the Holy Ghost represented.

I hadn't heard anything bad or good about the Holy Ghost, nor had I ever heard anyone criticize tongue-talking people. These things added up to a total void in my spiritual experience. I remember the first person who explained the scriptures to me. I wondered, "How did these scriptures get in the Bible?" I had read through the Bible many times, but I didn't remember any scriptures talking about the Holy Spirit. You can put on denominational eyeglasses that literally cause you to look at the Word and not see what the Spirit of God is saying.

People sometimes have the idea that praying in the Spirit is simply praying with an excited attitude, a heightened spiritual awareness, or with more intensity. Prayer in the Spirit is defined by Paul in 1 Corinthians 14.

Paul said, **"Pursue love...."** Immediately following that, he said, **"And desire spiritual gifts..."** (1 Corinthians 14:1). If we understand this verse properly, spiritual gifts are not for our own consumption. They are to bless other people. If you really love other people, you will want the supernatural power of the Holy Spirit to bring what is needed on the scene—the word of knowledge, the word of wisdom, discerning of spirits, the working of miracles, the gift of faith, the gifts of healings, or tongues, interpretation of tongues and prophecy.

161

Paul goes on in verse 1 to say, **"But especially that you may prophesy."** Prophecy is the anointed revelation word of God that comes by the Holy Spirit.

> **For he who speaks in a tongue does not speak to men but to God, for no one understands him; however, in the spirit he speaks mysteries.**
>
> **1 Corinthians 14:2**

When you are speaking in tongues, you are addressing God. You are speaking mysteries. Things that are not known in the natural will flow up out of you as you speak in the Spirit.

When you pray in tongues, you are speaking to God, but when you prophesy, you are speaking to men. When you are speaking in tongues, no one comprehends what is being said unless there is someone to interpret.

On the Day of Pentecost, the 120 in the upper room spoke in tongues and told the wondrous works of God. It was a sign and a wonder. It verified to them that God was in their midst. It opened their hearts for Peter to preach the great Pentecost message that Joel had prophesied of the latter-day outpouring of the Holy Spirit and that they should repent and believe on Jesus Christ. As a result, many were saved.

> **But he who prophesies speaks edification and exhortation and comfort to men.**
>
> **1 Corinthians 14:3**

People who don't believe in the gifts of the Spirit will always identify prophecy as inspired preaching, but prophecy is an anointed word that comes directly from God. Many can preach from God's Word, read a scripture, explain what it means and admonish the people to act on it, but it takes the operation of the gift of the Spirit to prophesy. Prophecy is a supernatural gift.

Edification means "to build up." To *exhort* is "to challenge someone to do what God has spoken." To *comfort* is "to minister the presence of the Holy Spirit in the mercy aspect of God."

162

Praying in Tongues
Edifies and Strengthens

He who speaks in a tongue edifies himself, but he who prophesies edifies the church.

1 Corinthians 14:4

Paul is drawing a contrast between prophecy and tongues. He is not saying to do away with tongues. Sometimes people say, "The Corinthians were one of the most sinful groups of people, and they had one of the most worldly churches. They operated in the gifts of the Spirit, and since Paul had to correct them, tongues aren't relevant for the Church today. Tongues are just for carnal churches."

They also took communion, so if you use the argument that tongues aren't necessary in the Church today, then you need to throw out communion, too. First Corinthians 11 gives instructions on communion. Many churches today have a problem understanding what God is saying. Paul wrote to explain communion, the gifts of the Spirit, the operation of love and how tongues and interpretation are to operate supernaturally in a church service.

When someone prophesies under the anointing of the Holy Spirit in a known language, everyone can understand it and be edified spiritually. Do you ever need to be built up? If you're not up, you're not going to help anyone else get up. If you're not spiritually strong, you will have difficulty ministering strength to other people. That's why praying in the Spirit in an unknown tongue is such an important part of our prayer life.

Paul is *not* saying, "Do away with tongues." This is what many people say who don't believe in tongues. First Corinthians 14:5 supports the argument that Paul was *not* discrediting tongues. *"I wish you all spoke with tongues...."*

In Mark 16:17, Jesus said, **"And these signs will follow those who believe...*they will speak with new tongues.*"**

Acts 2:4 says that the 120 in the upper room on the Day of Pentecost, which included Jesus' disciples, **"were all filled with the Holy Spirit and began to speak with other tongues, as the Spirit gave them utterance."**

Acts 10:44-46 indicates that the Holy Spirit fell on the Gentiles in Cornelius' household, and they spoke in tongues:

> **While Peter was still speaking these words, the Holy Spirit fell upon all those who heard the word.**
>
> **And those of the circumcision who believed were astonished, as many as came with Peter, because the gift of the Holy Spirit had been poured out on the Gentiles also.**
>
> **For they heard them speak with tongues and magnify God....**

In Acts 19:2-6, the disciples at Ephesus received the Holy Spirit as Paul laid his hands on them.

> **He said to them, "Did you receive the Holy Spirit when you believed?" So they said to him, "We have not so much as heard whether there is a Holy Spirit."**
>
> **And he said to them, "Into what then were you baptized?" So they said, "Into John's baptism."**
>
> **Then Paul said, "John indeed baptized with a baptism of repentance, saying to the people that they should believe on Him who would come after him, that is, on Christ Jesus."**
>
> **When they heard this, they were baptized in the name of the Lord Jesus.**
>
> **And when Paul had laid hands on them, the Holy Spirit came upon them, and they spoke with tongues and prophesied.**

In 1 Corinthians 14:5, Paul continues to explain the importance of speaking in tongues:

> **I wish you all spoke with tongues, but even more that you prophesied; for he who prophesies is greater than he who speaks with tongues, unless indeed he interprets, that the church may receive edification.**

Notice the phrase, **"unless indeed he interprets."** Prophecy is elevated over tongues in the public assembly, except when there is an interpretation. Tongues and interpretation are equivalent to prophecy.

Though people don't understand the "tongues" portion of tongues and interpretation, they will understand and be edified by the interpretation. The interpretation is a prophetic, supernatural utterance that comes from the Lord, and it will edify, exhort and comfort.

> **But now, brethren, if I come to you speaking with tongues, what shall I profit you unless I speak to you either by revelation, by knowledge, by prophesying, or by teaching?**
>
> **1 Corinthians 14:6**

Anyone who moves in the prophet's office can bring a revelation from God. Preaching and teaching are basically the dissemination, distribution, or impact of knowledge and doctrine, but Paul separates these. He says:

> **Even things without life, whether flute or harp, when they make a sound, unless they make a distinction in the sounds, how will it be known what is piped or played?**
>
> **For if the trumpet makes an uncertain sound, who will prepare for battle?**
>
> **So likewise you, unless you utter by the tongue words easy to understand, how will it be known what is spoken? For you will be speaking into the air.**
>
> **1 Corinthians 14:7-9**

If I speak a message to my congregation in tongues, I would be edified, but they would not be blessed. It would be like blowing an instrument, but there would be no distinction in the sounds, no harmony, no flow, no pattern and it would make no sense.

Paul was saying, "If a trumpet sounds a distinct sound that everyone recognizes as the sound for battle, they will prepare for it." He was emphasizing the importance of having an interpreter when a message is given in tongues. He wasn't saying to throw out tongues but to put tongues in its place.

> **There are, it may be, so many kinds of languages in the world, and none of them is without significance.**
>
> **Therefore, if I do not know the meaning of the language, I shall be a foreigner to him who speaks, and he who speaks will be a foreigner to me.**
>
> **Even so you, since you are zealous for spiritual gifts, let it be for the edification of the church that you seek to excel.**
>
> **Therefore let him who speaks in a tongue pray that he may interpret.**
>
> **1 Corinthians 14:10-13**

Paul was saying, "If you are so zealous of spiritual gifts, seek to edify, build up and strengthen the whole church." He didn't say, "Stop praying in tongues." He said, "If you are going to pray in tongues, pray for an interpretation, because when you have an interpretation, the whole church will be edified and blessed."

> **For if I pray in a tongue, my spirit prays, but my understanding is unfruitful.**
>
> **1 Corinthians 14:14**

Paul defined praying in the Spirit as praying in an unknown tongue. When you pray in tongues, you only have half a loaf, because your understanding is unfruitful.

166

What is the conclusion then? I will pray with the spirit, and I will also pray with the understanding. I will sing with the spirit, and I will also sing with the understanding.

1 Corinthians 14:15

Paul is encouraging believers to pray in their understanding and pray in the Spirit. Pray for interpretation when you pray in the Spirit, and you will move over into praying in your understanding and revelation will come.

Otherwise, if you bless with the spirit, how will he who occupies the place of the uninformed say "Amen" at your giving of thanks, since he does not understand what you say?

1 Corinthians 14:16

You can bless and give thanks to the Lord in the Spirit, but no one else will know what you are doing.

For you indeed give thanks well, but the other is not edified.

1 Corinthians 14:17

Praying in tongues is a proper, accepted and beneficial way to give thanks, but other people will not be edified without an interpretation.

I thank my God I speak with tongues more than you all.

1 Corinthians 14:18

Paul spoke in tongues more than the entire Corinthian bunch. Obviously, he wasn't saying, "Quit." He was saying, "I am doing it in the proper time personally and privately. I am speaking to God and giving thanks in the Spirit. I am communing with my Father and blessing Him. I am speaking mysteries unto Him."

Yet in the church I would rather speak five words with my understanding, that I may teach others also, than ten thousand words in a tongue.

1 Corinthians 14:19

167

Paul was saying, "When I stand up to minister, I would rather speak in a language you can understand than ten thousand words in an unknown tongue, because five words you can understand will help you more than ten thousand you can't understand."

We experienced this in our Russian crusades. I could preach all day to those people in English, and I would be blessed because of the Word coming forth, but they wouldn't comprehend a thing. A young man who speaks both Russian and English interpreted so the people could comprehend what I was saying.

Paul is saying, "I would that all of you spoke with tongues." You may be questioning, "Do you have to speak in tongues to go to heaven?" No. You must believe in Jesus Christ and believe in His shed blood, believe He died for you, He was raised from the dead, declare Him Lord and live out His lordship in your life.

You don't have to pray in tongues, tithe, serve the Lord in some type of Christian service, or praise and worship Him. But you will be blessed if you praise and worship the Lord. You will be blessed if you serve the Lord in a practical way in service to other people. You will be blessed if you give tithes and offerings. You will be blessed if you pray in the Spirit and in other tongues.

When we talk about praying in the Spirit, we are talking about the supernatural anointing and utterance in other tongues which builds you up. When you are built up, you can build other people up.

The Holy Spirit Helps Us Pray with Accuracy

Romans 8:26 KJV gives us another aspect of the importance of praying in the Spirit:

Likewise the Spirit also helpeth our infirmities: for we know not what we should pray for as we ought: but the Spirit itself [Himself] maketh intercession for us with groanings which cannot be uttered.

When Paul talks about *infirmities*, many people think he is referring to sickness and disease. In this verse, he is not talking about sickness and disease. *Infirmity*, as used in this verse, refers to weakness or natural, limited human ability. When we have areas where we lack, we don't understand, or we aren't capable of achieving in our natural ability, the Holy Spirit helps us. In other words, the Spirit of God will take hold in the area where we are weak and will strengthen us.

In verse 26, Paul identifies one area of weakness: *"For we do not know what we should pray for as we ought...."* There are two aspects of this thing: 1) We don't know what to pray for; and 2) We don't know how we ought to pray. Those are weaknesses or infirmities.

Some people offer a prayer like this: "God bless the president, my family, China, and Lord, reach Africa." After ten minutes, they are done, because they don't know what else to pray.

Paul is saying that it is a weakness (or infirmity) to not know what to pray for or how to pray, because God moves in response to our prayers. If we can't pray and we can't take hold of the blessing and power of God, there is a limitation.

Paul says, **"The Spirit Himself makes intercession for us with groanings which cannot be uttered"** (Romans 8:26). There are utterances that we won't know how to express in a known language. They will come out in another tongue as the Holy Spirit utters those things through us.

> **Now He who searches the hearts knows what the mind of the Spirit is, because He makes intercession for the saints according to the will of God.**
>
> **Romans 8:27**

The Spirit of God, Who dwells on the inside of you, will make the intercession if you allow Him to pray through you.

Remember, Paul said, **"If I pray in a tongue, my spirit prays..."** (1 Corinthians 14:14). In Romans 8:26, Paul is saying,

"The Spirit of God takes hold of our spirit, and utterances that cannot be expressed in our known language begin to flow out of us."

The Holy Spirit knows three vital things: 1) He knows your heart; 2) He knows God's heart; and 3) He knows all about the situation or person for whom you are praying. Not only does He know what to pray for, but He knows how to pray for it. His prayer won't be a hit and miss prayer. It will be according to the mind and will of the Father. It won't be contradictory to you, because the Holy Spirit is linked up with your spirit and knows your spirit. Therefore, when you pray in the Spirit, you are praying a prayer of perfection, a prayer of accuracy, a prayer of strength that you cannot pray in your weakened ability as a human being without the Holy Spirit's anointing, help, revelation, insight and utterance.

When you pray in the Spirit, you go beyond your natural limitations and pray according to the mind of the Father.

Praying in Tongues Brings
Rest and Refreshing

The prophet Isaiah spoke of the benefit of praying in another tongue:

**For with stammering lips and another tongue
He will speak to this people,**

**To whom He said, "This is the rest with which
you may cause the weary to rest," and, "This is the
refreshing...."**

Isaiah 28:11,12

Not only does praying in the Spirit build your faith, but it can move you into a place of rest and refreshing.

Built Up to Build Others Up!

Jude said:

170

> **But you, beloved, building yourselves up on your**
> **most holy faith, praying in the Holy Spirit.**
>
> **Verse 20**

When you pray in the Spirit, you build yourself up. It's not a selfish thing to be built up in your spirit man. People go to church on Sunday to hear a sermon to be built up. People read the Bible to be built up. People take time alone with God in prayer to be built up spiritually.

Jude says when you pray in the Spirit, you become stronger in your faith. We know that **"Faith comes by hearing, and hearing by the word of God"** (Romans 10:17).

The second aspect of what Jude was saying about praying in the Spirit is found in verse 21:

> **Keep yourselves in the love of God, looking for**
> **the mercy of our Lord Jesus Christ unto eternal life.**

When someone consistently prays in the Spirit, the Spirit of God keeps drawing him back to righteousness.

It's like a thermostat. If your thermostat is set and you open a door and hot air comes in, the thermostat will cause the air-conditioner to kick in to make the room cooler, even though hot air is coming in. Similarly, when the enemy brings something against your life to turn you off, turn you away, or get you off track, the Spirit of God—your internal thermostat—will kick in. When you pray in the Spirit, your spirit will rise up and throw off what the devil tries to bring against your life.

You will keep yourself in the love of God by praying in the Spirit, because you give place to the Spirit. You are communing with Him and giving the Holy Spirit the right to dominate your heart. When you pray for the interpretation, you are giving Him the right to dominate your mind, too.

Your spirit can be deflated when you listen to ungodly music or conversation or when you are in ungodly places. In other words, certain environments will grieve your spirit. Arguing,

171

strife, negativism and depressed and cynical attitudes will repress your spint.

The spirit of the world wants to bring your spirit down, because when you are down in your spirit, you aren't going to witness. You aren't going to be a shining light. You aren't going to let the love of God flow through you. Instead, you will hide your light under a bushel. But when you start praying in the Spirit, you will counter all the junk that's in the world. I believe we need this oil in our lamps!

When you look at the five wise and the five foolish virgins and the oil in their lamps or lack of it and the fact that the Holy Spirit is referred to as oil, there is a strong possibility that the anointing and power of the Holy Spirit could have been what Jesus was referring to when He spoke about keeping our lamps trimmed. One way we can allow that to happen is by praying in the Spirit. It will keep your faith built up, and it will help to keep you in the love of God.

If you don't read the Word, which keeps your faith built up, praying in the Spirit won't automatically compensate for failure in this area or in any other area. In the same way, in keeping yourself in the love of God, if the Spirit of God prompts you to quit doing something and you don't obey, it won't produce the end result that is desired.

Jesus said:

"If anyone thirsts, let him come to Me and drink.

"He who believes in Me, as the Scripture has said, out of his heart will flow rivers of living water."

This He spoke concerning the Spirit, whom those believing in Him would receive; for the Holy Spirit was not yet given, because Jesus was not yet glorified.

John 7:37-39

Rivers of living water out of your innermost being refer to
the flow of the Spirit of God. A part of that flow is the prayer
language of the Spirit. Isaiah called it "stammering lips, another
tongue, a rest and a refreshing."

In Ephesians 6:18, the final piece of the believer's armor that
is mentioned is, **"Praying always with all prayer and supplication in the Spirit...."** Praying in the Spirit is very specifically
defined in Scripture as "praying in other tongues."

When you are edified by praying in the Spirit, you can edify
other people. As you go with the flow of the Holy Spirit, God will
quicken you to pray for others.

Years ago, the Holy Spirit kept bringing someone to my mind
for whom I was to pray. I had gone through twelve years of school
with this guy. During one of my college breaks when I went home
to Magnolia, Arkansas, I went out on the college track to run. The
man for whom I had been praying was running around the track,
too. He is now a medical doctor, and he just happened to be home
and at the track at the same time I was. I had an opportunity to
share Jesus Christ with him. At the time, though he didn't accept
Jesus Christ as his Lord and Savior, he was responsive.

Years later, when he was visiting family in Colorado, he
called me on the phone after seeing our TV program on Trinity
Broadcasting Network. Since then he has become a committed
Christian.

Along with the other benefits of praying in the Spirit, you
will be strengthened in boldness to witness as you pray in other
tongues.

Gospel Prayer Truths

Here are fifteen gospel prayer truths from Chapter 12:

1. When you pray in the Spirit, you are speaking to God (1 Corinthians 14:2).

2. The person who prophesies brings edification, exhortation and comfort to others.

3. Prophecy is an anointed word that comes directly from God.

4. As you pray in tongues, you will edify or strengthen your inner man (1 Corinthians 14:4).

5. If you are spiritually strong, you can minister strength to other people.

6. One of the signs Jesus said would follow believers is they would speak with new tongues (Mark 16:17).

7. When you pray in tongues, you should ask the Holy Spirit to help you interpret (1 Corinthians 14:13). In this way, you will receive revelation.

8. When you pray in tongues, other people will not be edified unless there is an interpretation (1 Corinthians 14:16,17).

9. When you don't know what to pray, the Holy Spirit will help you (Romans 8:26). He knows what to pray for and how to pray for it.

10. When you pray in the Spirit, you are praying a prayer of perfection, accuracy and strength.

11. When you pray in the Spirit, you go beyond your natural limitations and pray according to the mind of the Father.

12. Praying in the Spirit will move you into a place of rest and refreshing (Isaiah 28:11,12).

13. To pray in the Spirit and be built up will help you to walk in love (Jude 20,21).

14. When you pray in the Spirit, your spirit will rise up and throw off what the devil tries to bring against your life.

15. You will be strengthened in boldness to witness as you pray in other tongues.

QUESTIONS

Part 1. Completion
Please complete each of the statements.

1. Prophecy is the anointed ___ _____ word of God that comes by the Holy Spirit.

2. Paul says the person who prays in tongues is speaking to _____ rather than to men (1 Corinthians 14:2).

3. Prophecy brings one or more of what three things to the hearer, according to 1 Corinthians 14:3?

    a. _____

    b. _____

    c. _____

4. Paul said, "He who speaks in a tongue edifies _____, but he who prophesies edifies the _____" (1 Corinthians 14:4).

5. When the 120 were filled with the Holy Spirit on the Day of Pentecost, Scripture says they spoke with _____ _____ as the Spirit gave them utterance (Acts 2:4).

6. When the Gentiles in Cornelius' household were filled with the Holy Spirit, they spoke in _____ and _____ God (Acts 10:44-46).

7. Tongues and interpretation are equivalent to _____.

8. When we don't know how to appropriately pray for a person or a situation, Paul says, "The Spirit Himself makes _____ for us with groanings which cannot be uttered" (Romans 8:26).

9. The prophet Isaiah said _____ and _____ would come as a result of praying in tongues (Isaiah 28:11,12).

10. When a Spirit-filled person quits praying in tongues, he or she also quits walking in _____.

11. The "rivers of living water" which Jesus spoke of in John 7:38 refer to the flow of the _____ of God through a believer's life.

12. Another benefit of praying in the Spirit is that you will be bold to _____ to others.

Part 2. Personal Application

Please complete the questions and/or statements to the best of your ability.

1. Sorne of the benefits I have experienced from praying in the Spirit and asking for interpretation are

   _____

   _____

   _____

   _____

2. I experienced the rest and refreshing from praying in the Spirit which Isaiah spoke of when _____

   _____

   _____

   _____

   _____

3. Some of the ways I keep myself built up spiritually are by

   _____

   _____

   _____

   _____

CHAPTER 13

THE PRAYER OF PRAISE AND THANKSGIVING

When we praise and worship God, we are in communion and fellowship with Him. We're not just spectators standing on the sidelines or up in the grandstands praising someone unrelated to us, but we are in vital union with Him.

The prayer of praise and thanksgiving should be incorporated with all the other types of prayer.

Paul said in Ephesians 1:3:

Blessed be the God and Father of our Lord Jesus Christ, who has blessed us with every spiritual blessing in the heavenly places in Christ.

That means everything we need to live our lives victoriously has already been provided through the death, burial and resurrection of Jesus Christ. God's blessings have already come to us in Christ Jesus. We receive those blessings as we take a position in faith.

We know that the people who walk in the counsel of the Lord are blessed.

Blessed is the man who walks not in the counsel of the ungodly, nor stands in the path of sinners, nor sits in the seat of the scornful;

But his delight is in the law of the Lord, and in His law he meditates day and night.

He shall be like a tree planted by the rivers of water, that brings forth its fruit in its season,

**whose leaf also shall not wither; and whatever he
does shall prosper.**

Psalm 1:1-3

There are specific things we must do to inherit the blessings
of God, but everything that we need has already been provided.
Peter spoke the same thing from a different viewpoint:

As His divine power has given to us *all things*
that pertain to life and godliness, **through the**
knowledge of Him who called us by glory and
virtue.

2 Peter 1:3

According to this scripture, God has already given us everything that pertains to life and godliness. Verse 4 contains the key
to obtaining the things God has already provided.

By which have been given to us exceedingly great
and precious promises, that through these you may
be partakers of the divine nature, having escaped
the corruption that is in the world through lust.

It is through *the promises in God's Word* that we partake of
what God has already provided. So how do we get it out of the
realm of the unseen world into our everyday lives? God reveals
what He has provided *through His great and precious promises.*

That's why our prayer lives must be wrapped around the
promises of God. When the revelation of what God has done for
us comes to us, then we must take the promises, stand on them,
believe them, declare them and God will bring them to pass in
our lives.

When you were born again, I'm sure you heard John 3:16:

"For God so loved the world that He gave His
only begotten Son, that whoever believes in Him
should not perish but have everlasting life."

Jesus went to the cross and paid for our sin, sickness and

poverty 2,000 years ago. He's not going to the cross again. Redemption and eternal life have already been provided, but when do you find out about it? When someone relates that truth to you, or when you hear it through the Word. To the degree that you believe and obey the Word, you receive what God has already provided.

One of the greatest things you can do is get books that contain the promises of God, and take your Bible and note every promise that God has written down. Then thank God for His promises.

Paul said:

But thanks be to God, who gives us the victory through our Lord Jesus Christ.

1 Corinthians 15:57

The prayer of faith incorporates praise worship and thanksgiving. If your prayer of faith doesn't end in praise, worship and thanksgiving, then it really isn't the prayer of faith.

Philippians 4:6,7 TLB says:

Don't worry about anything; instead, pray about everything; tell God your needs and *don't forget to thank him for his answers.*

If you do this you will experience God's peace, which is far more wonderful than the human mind can understand. His peace will keep your thoughts and your hearts quiet and at rest as you trust in Christ Jesus.

How can you make a prayer *with thanksgiving* if you don't know it is going to come to pass? We must believe God's promise in 1 John 5:14,15:

Now this is the confidence that we have in Him, that if we ask anything according to His will, He hears us.

And if we know that He hears us, whatever we

ask, we know that we have the petitions that we have asked of Him.

Jesus said in Mark 11:24:

Therefore I say to you, whatever things you ask when you pray, believe that you receive them, and you will have them.

If you believe that you receive when you pray, when should you give thanks? The moment you offer your prayer! Offer it with thanksgiving and praise, and begin to worship God for the answer, incorporating an attitude that acknowledges that God has already provided everything you need.

Hebrews 13:15 says:

Therefore by Him let us continually offer the sacrifice of praise to God, that is, the fruit of our lips, *giving thanks to His name.*

Paul said, **"Rejoice in the Lord always. Again I will say, rejoice!"** (Philippians 4:4). In 1 Thessalonians 5:18, Paul said, **"In everything give thanks...."** How can you give thanks in everything unless you believe that God has already provided everything you need? That regardless of what happens in the natural, God has already made full provision for you? Once you understand this, then you can offer prayers that are filled with praise.

One of the ways the Lord helped me understand this in my life was when I was flying a small plane years ago. You taxi down the runway, but you aren't off the ground until the point of liftoff. The Lord said to me, "A lot of people are taxiing in their prayer life. They are just taxiing around the runway. They haven't lifted off the ground yet! They are going through the motions in prayer. They may even be checking the ailerons, the flaps, the wheels and the gauges, but there is no liftoff."

There comes a time when you have to lift the nose of that plane and accelerate. Then it comes off the ground! It's the same way in your prayer and praise life. There is a time when you must accelerate, lift your wings and begin to praise God for the manifestation of His promises. You say, "I don't feel like it." Your feelings have nothing to do with it! It's your faith that will make the difference.

Stay Jesus-Focused and Promise-Focused!

Paul gave the Philippians a key on how to stay focused after offering their prayers and praise. It's a key for us, too.

Fix your thoughts on what is true and good and right. Think about things that are pure and lovely, and dwell on the fine, good things in others. Think about all you can praise God for and be glad about.

Philippians 4:8 TLB

What you think about during the time frame of your prayers and praise and the manifestation of your answers will determine whether you receive or not. The battle has to be won in your mind. See your answers coming to pass. Many people lose the battle in their imagination. They don't see it coming to pass.

Many people say, "What you say is what you will have." I want to add something to that: "What you *see* is also what you will have," because what you see in your mind will ultimately affect what you say. That's why the enemy comes with lying imaginations.

Thank God for His promise in 2 Corinthians 10:3-5:

For though we walk in the flesh, we do not war according to the flesh.

For the weapons of our warfare are not carnal but mighty in God for pulling down strongholds,

Casting down arguments (*The King James Version* says **"imaginations"**) **and every high thing that exalts itself against the knowledge of God,**

bringing every thought into captivity to the obedience of Christ.

The victory over the enemy has already been won for us through Jesus Christ. Jesus has already been raised high above the wicked spirits and principalities that are in the heavenly places. He is the Head and we are the Body, so we are not *under* the authority of the demonic principalities and powers. We are *above* their authority, because Ephesians 2:6 says God has *"raised us up together, and made us sit together in the heavenly places in Christ Jesus."*

How do we then come against the wicked spirits that are in heavenly places? Through believing the Word of God, through the name of Jesus Christ and through the power of Jesus' shed blood. All of those agree: the name, the Word and the blood.

I recall a person sharing on a tape how he had visited a church where the minister said, "Let's all stand. We're going to punch out the devil." As the people stood, he said they all got into a boxing stance, and they began to punch out the devil. The person on the tape said, "I think they were sincere in what they were doing, but I don't think they have a revelation of what Jesus has already done."

Do you know that we are not sending the devil to hell? People will pray that, but the devil has never been there. He is going there, and one day he will be in the lake of fire. He will be bound for a thousand years, but we are not going to do it. The archangel, Michael, is going to do it.

Some of the teachings on spiritual warfare in regard to prayer are coming from people who don't have a revelation of what Christ has already done. When you understand that your body is the temple of the Holy Spirit and you don't get into bitterness, resentment and unforgiveness, the Bible says you will give the devil no place (Ephesians 4:27).

You can't cast out, kick out, vomit out, or beat out the bitterness, resentment, or unforgiveness that is in a person. The person needs forgiveness, not deliverance. There have been times when I have seen people beat on someone and scream, "We command that thing to come out." Many times when I encounter this type of situation, God will give me a word of knowledge, and I'll ask the person, "Have you forgiven _____ ?" In such a case, if they will forgive, they will be set free.

The fiery darts of the devil that come at Christians are usually thoughts, feelings and imaginations that come to the soulish realm. They will work through the flesh to try to arouse the lust of the flesh, the lust of the eyes and the pride of life, but you can defeat them by *believing the Bible*.

In spiritual warfare, two of the greatest things you can do that will stop the devil are to *believe the Bible* and *praise God for what He has already done*. That is warfare, because the weapons of our warfare are not carnal. The strongholds we are pulling down are in people's minds. To pull down the thoughts and imaginations that have become strongholds in your mind, renew your mind to what God has already done through Jesus Christ, and start praising God for His Word.

What happens when we believe the Bible—when we believe the promises of God? *God performs His Word.* God says in Jeremiah 1:12, **"I am ready to perform My word."**

We must become Jesus-focused and promise-focused rather than problem-focused. Keep the Word in your mouth rather than the world. Declare what God has done rather than what the devil is doing. Focus on light rather than darkness.

You can stand in a dark room all day and say, "Darkness, I command you to get out of here." You can roll on the floor, scream, beat and get a hundred people agreeing for the darkness to go. One six year old can come in and flip on the light switch and the darkness will go. If one person will believe the Word, he can put thousands of the enemy's works and effects on people's lives to flight in one moment.

Jesus said, **"If you have faith as a mustard seed, you will say to this mountain, 'Move from here to there,' and it will move; and nothing will be impossible for you"** (Matthew 17:20). Jesus said in John 14:30 KJV, **"The prince of this world cometh, and *hath nothing in me*."**

Prayer is simply agreeing with what God has already done. It is taking His Word—His promises—and saying, "Father, according to Your Word, You have redeemed me from the curse. Thank You, Father, that my steps are ordered by You." That's a prayer of praise and thanksgiving. "Thank You, Father, that I am Your sheep. You said Your sheep would hear Your voice. I refuse to hear the voice of a stranger."

I deal with people who have been praying for years, trying to cast the devil's thoughts out of their mind. "Please pray for me. I have these harassing thoughts," they often say. If they would spend just five minutes a day confessing and acknowledging that they do not hear the voice of a stranger, but they only hear the voice of the Good Shepherd, their life could be radically turned around. When you accentuate the positive, you will eliminate the negative! When you turn the light on, the darkness goes. Keep the sword of the Spirit in your mouth, declaring it daily.

If a person sins, he needs to repent. If a person has been ugly, he needs to get it out of his life. I am not talking about just confessing sin and not dealing with it.

When a person confesses, "God meets all of my needs," that doesn't mean he goes and lays on a park bench and waits for the money to fall off the oak tree! When you are confessing for a good mate, it doesn't mean you don't take a shower or brush your teeth in three days. You need to be the kind of person that you are looking for.

If you are confessing healing, you don't go swimming in Minnesota in January. You would have to cut a hole in the ice to do it, and that wouldn't make a lot of sense! In other words, when you confess God's Word and thank Him for His Word, there are *corresponding actions* that must be matched up with the confession.

Habakkuk had something to say about praising God regardless of natural circumstances.

> **Although the fig tree shall not blossom, neither shall fruit be in the vines; the labour of the olive shall fail, and the fields shall yield no meat; the flock shall be cut off from the fold, and there shall be no herd in the stalls:**
>
> **Yet I will rejoice in the Lord, I will joy in the God of my salvation.**
>
> **The Lord God is my strength, and he will make my feet like hinds' feet, and he will make me to walk upon mine high places....**
>
> **Habakkuk 3:17-19 KJV**

We can rejoice in the midst of our circumstances, because God is our strength—not the economy of the nation or what is happening in the natural.

Since God is our Shepherd and strength, He will do something for us regardless of natural circumstances. He will cause us to ride upon the high places of the earth, as Isaiah prophesied:

> **Then shalt thou delight thyself in the Lord; and I will cause thee to ride upon the high places of the earth, and feed thee with the heritage of Jacob thy father: for the mouth of the Lord hath spoken it.**
>
> **Isaiah 58:14 KJV**

When Jonah was in the whale s belly and took that Mediterrnean cruise, he said:

> **"When I had lost all hope, I turned my thoughts once more to the Lord. And my earnest prayer went to you in your holy Temple.**
>
> **"(Those who worship false gods have turned**

their backs on all the mercies waiting for them
from the Lord!)

"I will never worship anyone but you! For how
can I thank you enough for all you have done? I
will surely fulfill my promises. For my deliverance
comes from the Lord alone."

And the Lord ordered the fish to spit up Jonah
on the beach, and it did.

Jonah 2:7-10 TLB

As Jonah thanked and praised the Lord, he was delivered
from the whale's belly!

Prayers of praise and thanksgiving will bring God's hand of
deliverance on the scene in your behalf! Prayers of praise and
thanksgiving should be a part of your daily lifestyle!

Gospel Prayer Truths

Here are fourteen gospel prayer truths from Chapter 13:

1. When you praise and worship God, you are in communion
   and fellowship with Him.

2. In Christ Jesus, God has given us everything that pertains
   to life and godliness. We partake of His blessings through
   acting upon the promises of His Word (2 Peter 1:3,4).

3. Our prayer lives must be wrapped around the promises of
   God, because in the promises of His Word is everything
   we will ever need.

4. To the degree that you *believe* and *obey* God's Word, you
   will receive God's provision.

5. The prayer of faith incorporates praise, worship and
   thanksgiving.

6. Faith thanks God for His answers to your prayers *the
   moment you pray.*

7. You will have continual praise to God upon your lips as you meditate upon the things which are true, good, right, pure and lovely (Philippians 4:8 TLB).

8. The greatest thing you can do to stop the devil is believe the Bible and start *praising* God for what He already has done.

9. To remain Jesus-focused and promise-focused rather than problem-focused will bring God on the scene in your behalf.

10. If you have faith as a grain of mustard seed, nothing will be impossible to you (Matthew 17:20).

11. Prayer is agreeing with what God has already done.

12. When you accentuate the positive in your words and prayers, the negative will be eliminated.

13. When you pray and confess God's Word, there are natural corresponding actions you must take.

14. Prayers of praise and thanksgiving will loose God's hand of deliverance.

QUESTIONS

Part 1. Completion

Please complete each of the statements.

1. According to Ephesians 1:3, we have already been "blessed...
    with every _____ _____ in the
    heavenly places in Christ."

2. According to Psalm 1:1-3, the person who is blessed is one
    who _____ in God's Word day and night.
    Whatever he or she does will _____.

3. Second Peter 1 :3 says everything has already been given to
    us that pertains to _____ and _____.
    We partake of what God has provided through the
    _____ of His Word.

4. To the degree that you _____ and _____ the
    Word, you will receive what God has provided.

5. Philippians 4:6 TLB says, "Tell God your needs and don't
    forget to _____ him for his answers." As a result of
    being thankful, verse 7 says, "You will experience God's
    _____."

6. Jesus said in Mark 11:24, "Whatever things you ask when
    you pray, believe that you _____ them,
    and you will have them."

7. Philippians 4:8 TLB gives instruction for focusing your
    thoughts. The seven kinds of thoughts Paul says to focus on
    are:

    a. _____

    b. _____

    c. _____

    d._____

    e. _____

190

     f. _____

     g. _____

8. Two of the greatest things you can do to stop the devil in spiritual warfare are:

     a. _____

     b. _____

9. In Matthew 17:20 Jesus said if you have faith as a mustard seed, _____ will be impossible for you.

10. Natural corresponding _____ must be matched up with your confessions.

11. Isaiah 58:14 says God will cause the person who delights in Him to ride upon the _____ _____ of the earth.

12. To bring God on the scene in our lives, we must be Jesus-focused and promise-focused rather than _____ focused.

Part 2. Personal Application

Please complete the questions and/or statements to the best of your ability.

1. I live and walk in the counsel of the Lord by _____

_____

_____

_____

_____

2. I will stay Jesus-focused and promise-focused rather than problem-focused by _____

_____

_____

_____

_____

3. I will cooperate with the Holy Spirit in guarding what I hear, see and say by _____

_____

_____

_____

_____

4. I offer the fruit of my lips in thanksgiving and praise to the Lord, which is a consistent part of my lifestyle, as follows:

_____

_____

_____

_____

_____

CHAPTER 14

PRAYING FOR FAMILY SALVATION

The same principles of praying for family salvation presented in this chapter are applicable in praying for the lost of any community, culture, or nation.

Jesus said, **"Heaven and earth will pass away, but My words will by no means pass away"** (Matthew 24:35). Holy men of God spoke as they were moved by the Holy Ghost, so what is written in God's Word is not just the will or whim of man, but it is the revelation of God coming through men so we might know God's will and purpose in the earth.

When we base our prayers on God's unchanging promises, we will receive His answers to our prayers. Acts 16:31 says:

> **Believe on the Lord Jesus Christ, and you will be saved, you and your household.**

If you are a born-again believer, God has given you a promise in this verse that your family members will also believe and confess Jesus Christ as their Lord and Savior.

God loves families. He started with Adam and Eve. It was His plan that they have children, subdue the earth and take dominion over it. Although they had a problem in their home, with one son killing another, that didn't stop God. He raised up another righteous seed.

The knowledge of God was passed on to Noah. During Noah's day, all the people around him rejected God. They absolutely refused Him. Nothing could reach them, so God said, **"I will destroy man whom I have created from the face of the**

earth, both man and beast, creeping thing and birds of the
air, for I am sorry that I have made them" (Genesis 6:7), This
is a type and shadow of what will ultimately happen to people
who live in the world today who reject God. God destroyed all the
inhabitants of the earth through a flood, except for Noah and his
seed. "Noah found grace in the eyes of the Lord" (v. 8).

God promised He would not destroy the earth again with a
flood, but He spoke in the Word through Peter that there would
be an everlasting fire for those who reject Jesus Christ.

The good news is, seven days before the flood, after building
the ark, the word of the Lord came to Noah to gather his family
and enter into the ark.

> "Come into the ark, you and all your household,
> because I have seen that you are righteous before
> Me in this generation...
>
> "For after seven more days I will cause it to rain
> on the earth forty days and forty nights, and I will
> destroy from the face of the earth all living things
> that I have made."
>
> **Genesis 7:1,4**

The Bible doesn't say a lot about Noah's family being righteous, but it says Noah was righteous. He believed God and built
an ark in obedience to God's directions. Obviously, his wife and
kids helped him during those many years of construction. They
believed and entered the ark under Noah's leadership.

When the final penalty for all the wicked is released from
God and the final judgment day is gone, I am believing that your
family will be in the ark of salvation.

Most people have some folks in their family that they don't
know if they are the kind of people God even wants to save!
Maybe some of your family have wondered about you, too! Be
encouraged about your family's salvation.

God chose Abraham and said He was going to bless him and

194

through him, He would bless the families of the earth (Genesis 12:1-3). He blessed him with a son, Isaac, who had a son named Jacob. Jacob had twelve sons who became the twelve tribes of Israel. God is interested in families, and His blessing extends outward to your relatives. The blessing of God includes the salvation of every member of your family.

First Timothy 2:4 says God **"desires all men to be saved and to come to the knowledge of the truth."** That includes your family members and relatives! "All men" means *all of the human race*. It is God's will that every man, woman, boy and girl be saved.

Not everyone is going to be saved, but that does not change the will of God. He sent Jesus to die on the cross, to be buried and raised from the dead so *"whoever* **calls on the name of the Lord shall be saved"** (Romans 10:13).

Second Peter 3:9 says:

> **The Lord is not slack concerning His promise, as some count slackness, but is longsuffering toward us, not willing that any should perish but that all should come to repentance.**

The reason Jesus hasn't already come is because of His mercy. He is longsuffering, and He doesn't want anyone to be lost, so He is speaking to us to reach out and share His love with others.

Looking back through history, we know there are people who did not respond to the gospel, but that doesn't change God's will for all people to be saved. Remember, it was God's will that Adam and Eve be obedient, replenish the earth and take dominion. They violated God's will, so we have to understand that though men may fail, it does not change the will of God.

"Open Their Eyes To See You, Lord"

Second Corinthians 4:4 tells us that the god of this world

[Satan] has blinded the minds of those **"who do not believe, lest the light of the gospel of the glory of Christ, who is the image of God, should shine on them** [and they would believe on Jesus Christ]." The spiritual blindness Paul is speaking about in this verse keeps people from seeing the truth.

The good news is, you, as a believer, have authority and power to pray for the blindness to be removed. In praying for the church at Ephesus, Paul said, "I pray for the eyes of your understanding to be enlightened" (Ephesians 1:18). In other words, he was praying that the lights would come on in your house! If the spiritual lights are out in someone's life, you can pray for the blindness to be removed and for the light to shine in, in Jesus' name.

A few years ago, a lady in our church began to pray for her grandmother who had grown up in a denominational church but never knew the reality of having a personal relationship with Jesus Christ.

Here is the testimony of her grandmother's salvation experience:

"My grandmother played the piano in the silent movie theaters when they first started. After I got saved, I had a hard time witnessing to her, but I prayed for her.

"When I came to O.R.U., I wrote her an occasional letter and shared about what the Lord was doing in my life. When I went home to visit, I always shared positive things about the ministry and what the Lord was doing.

"One day as I was praying for her, a fervency came in me that I had not known for some sixteen years in praying for her. I was determined all day long that I would call her that night and lead her to Jesus.

"When I got home from church, I called her and said, 'Grandma, what are you doing?' She said, 'I am reading a *Guidepost Magazine,* and I need the Lord.' I said, 'I know, Grandma. That's why I called.'

196

"She hadn't heard the plan of salvation all her ninety-one years, but as I led her in a salvation prayer, she was born again. After I prayed with her, she said, 'I feel so clean. Now I don't have to go to hell.'"

Don't give up, no matter how old the people are for whom you are praying. Prayer based upon God's Word will prevail!

After His resurrection, Jesus walked on the road to Emmaus with two of His disciples who didn't recognize Him.

> **Now it came to pass, as He sat at the table with them, that He took bread, blessed and broke it, and gave it to them.**
>
> **Then their eyes were opened and they knew Him....**
>
> **Luke 24:30,31**

You can pray this passage over the lost: "Lord Jesus, open their eyes to know You."

Verse 45 of this same chapter says Jesus opened the eyes of the disciples to understand the scriptures that prophesied His resurrection.

If we will mix faith with God's promises, believing and speaking them, God will perform them. He will fulfill His promises.

Acts 2:17 says, **"And it shall come to pass in the last days, says God, that I will pour out of My Spirit on all flesh; your sons and your daughters shall prophesy, your young men shall see visions, your old men shall dream dreams."** Mix faith with this promise that your sons and daughters will prophesy, and hold fast to it.

Proverbs 11:21 KJV says, **"The seed of the righteous shall be delivered."**

Isaiah 60:1-4 says:

> **Arise, shine; for your light has come! And the glory of the Lord is risen upon you.**
>
> **For behold, the darkness shall cover the earth,**

and deep darkness the people; but the Lord will arise over you, and His glory will be seen upon you.

The Gentiles shall come to your light, and kings to the brightness of your rising.

Lift up your eyes all around, and see: they all gather together, they come to you; your sons shall come from afar, and your daughters shall be nursed at your side.

To mix faith with these promises, begin to declare:

Father, thank You that Your Word says the seed of the righteous will be delivered. You made me righteous by Your blood, not by my own works, but by the gift of righteousness. My children are delivered, in the name of Jesus. They are set free. Lord, You said my sons and daughters would be nursed at my side. Thank You for the privilege of nurturing them with Your Word.

Thank You, Father, for pouring Your Spirit out upon my seed—my sons and daughters. Your Word will never depart from their mouth, from the mouth of their children, or from the mouth of their children's children.

You can put agreement with Acts 2:4 for your children to be filled with the Holy Spirit, with the evidence of speaking in other tongues. **"And they were all filled with the Holy Spirit and began to speak with other tongues, as the Spirit gave them utterance."**

In Mark 16:15-18, Jesus said:

"Go into all the world and preach the gospel to every creature.

"He who believes and is baptized will be saved; but he who does not believe will be condemned.

"And these signs will follow those who believe: In My name they will cast out demons; they will speak with new tongues;

"They will take up serpents; and if they drink

anything deadly, it will by no means hurt them; they will lay hands on the sick, and they will recover."

Whenever Jesus gave a commission to go out and share the gospel, He also gave authority to cast out devils. Satan is the god of this world, and he has blinded the minds of the lost, keeping them from seeing the truth. You can loose the power of the Holy Spirit upon unbelievers, and bind the power of the devil and the wicked spirits off of them, in Jesus' name. You can take authority and command the wicked spirits to leave them and stand against the powers of darkness, even if the person is miles from you.

As believers in Jesus Christ, we have authority to pray and command the wicked spirits that have held people captive to be removed. Jesus said, **"How can one enter a strong man's house and plunder his goods, unless he first binds the strong man? And then he will plunder his house"** (Matthew 12:29).

We have to take authority over the strong man who has tried to wrap himself around a person's life and hold them back from salvation. We have been given authority to break the bands of the enemy and loose the captives. Many times people understand the principle of binding the devil only in relationship to some type of demonic oppression, but we need to see it in relationship to soulwinning.

When Sharon and I first went to Leningrad (now St. Petersburg), Russia, to hold crusades, we bound the strong spirits of religion from the people so when we gave an altar call, they would be free to respond.

When we go into the apartment communities to hold crusades in Tulsa and the surrounding area, we break the spirits of drugs, alcoholism, abuse and torment. Before the people ever come to the crusade, we pray that they will be free to respond to the gospel.

Loose a Spirit of Repentance

The Holy Spirit will convict of sin and reveal Jesus Christ to people. Pray for a spirit of repentance to be loosed over the lost.

And a servant of the Lord must not quarrel but be gentle to all, able to teach, patient,

In humility correcting those who are in opposition, if God perhaps will grant them repentance, so that they may know the truth,

And that they may come to their senses and escape the snare of the devil, having been taken captive by him to do his will.

2 Timothy 2:24-26

Unless a person repents and turns around, they won't be saved. They must have a heart change. When we pray for it, God will give repentance in people's lives.

Pray for Jesus To Be Lifted Up

Jesus said, **"And I, if I am lifted up from the earth, will draw all peoples to Myself"** (John 12:32).

We know Jesus was speaking about His death on the cross, but many people have never had Jesus Christ lifted up in their mind. They have not been introduced to the real Jesus. They have seen religion, denominationalism, ideas and hypocrisy. When they see the real Jesus lifted up above the fog of what man has said about Him, they will accept Him. The devil has blinded them from seeing Jesus' love and from understanding what the cross is all about.

You can pray, "Father, help _____ to know that there is no greater love than Jesus' love when He paid the ultimate price with His life so they wouldn't have to go to hell."

John 6:44 says, **"No one can come to Me unless the Father who sent Me draws him...."** You can pray, "Father, draw _____ with the cords of Your love. Mighty Holy Spirit, come upon _____'s life, in Jesus' name."

Months ago, in the days that followed a Sunday morning
200

illustrated sermon, Sharon and I received a note about one woman's deliverance from satanic bondage:

"About a year ago, my daughter's Grandma came to visit. As a child she had received Christ, but later she was sexually molested by her father. She got away from the church, went to college and earned two master's degrees in education. She lived in California and had become involved in a cult.

"We brought her to church at Victory Christian Center when you had an illustrated sermon about the servant who was forgiven by the king, who, in turn, wouldn't forgive his fellow servant.

"When you gave the altar call, she went forward and dedicated her life to Christ, forgave her father and was filled with the Holy Spirit."

This woman had never seen an illustrated sermon. It affected her to the point that she returned to her home in California and quit the cult.

You may be in a situation where you have family members who are on drugs or involved in a cult. God's power can break through those things. Don't give up on your loved ones.

Pray for Laborers

You can pray for laborers to cross the paths of the lost.

Then Jesus went about all the cities and villages, teaching in their synagogues, preaching the gospel of the kingdom, and healing every sickness and every disease among the people.

But when He saw the multitudes, He was moved with compassion for them, because they were weary and scattered, like sheep having no shepherd.

Then He said to His disciples, "The harvest truly is plentiful, but the laborers are few.

"Therefore pray the Lord of the harvest to send out laborers into His harvest."

Matthew 9:35-38

Your relatives and friends are part of God's harvest. To pray laborers across their pathways, you can declare: "Lord, send them tracts, books, tapes, videos, people, billboards, bumper stickers and radio and television programs. Every time they turn on the television, Lord, let the preacher point his finger at them and tell them, 'Get saved.' When they tune in the radio, Lord, let it stop where someone is preaching the gospel of Jesus Christ. Thank You, Father, that they are hearing a witness of Your Word."

Sharon's mother worked on me. She was our youth leader at church, and she kept giving me books. Then the little tract, "The Four Spiritual Laws," came to me. It was a little laborer that worked in my heart. Every time I picked it up and read it, it preached to me:

- God loves you.
- Sin has separated you from God.
- Jesus died for your sins.
- You must receive Jesus Christ.

Years ago when I was in state college, my roommate wasn't saved. At first he wouldn't listen to me, but finally at night he would say, "Put a towel under the door so nobody will know what we are doing. Talk real low and you can read the Bible to me." So, with a flashlight I read the Bible to him. He was 6'3", weighed 225 pounds, and was a defensive end on the football team. He didn't receive Christ at that time, but he listened as I read the Word.

One time we took him to a small group meeting off campus where everybody held hands as they prayed. The holding hands business, singing, clapping and sharing testimonies got to him, so that was the last time he attended a small group meeting with us.

After I transferred to O.R.U., one day as Sharon and her brother were going across the state college campus where I had attended, he yelled to them, "Praise the Lord!" That's what we always said to him, and he would respond, "Yeah, yeah, yeah." But this time he said it! He had committed his life to Jesus Christ!

In the monthly crusades we held in the government-subsidized apartment communities in our city, many times a resident would come up to us and say, "We have been praying, 'God, send a revival to our apartment community.'"

When we set up the crusade tent in Plaza Hills East, a lady shared with us, "Since I moved here almost a year and a half ago, I have prayed every day, 'God, send a revival into Plaza Hills East.'" She said, "As I walked across this piece of ground, I had a vision of a tent sitting out here." She didn't even know about our tent. She said, "As I prayed, I could see people walking all over these grounds witnessing."

The wonderful thing is, during our Friday night and Saturday afternoon crusade meetings, we had people going door to door witnessing, and the tent was set up right where this woman saw it in a vision. As we pray for laborers, God will send them.

When I was eleven years old, I mowed yards. The first yard I mowed was that of Millie, a beauty shop owner. My dad left the lawn mower there in the morning on his way to work, and I'd ride my bicycle over during the day and mow it. Then after work, Dad picked up the lawn mower, and I would take the money! It was a good deal! It kept me out of trouble, and Dad called that my allowance. It helped him out, too!

Although Millie's husband was a very intelligent construction worker, traveling across the country, he was a drunkard. His three sons were state champion tennis players, and in spite of the terrible situation at home, they all became doctors and medical professionals. Sometimes this family went for four or five years without hearing from their father.

Millie began to hear that she could pray for her husband to be saved, so she began to pray for Reuben.

In 1976 when Sharon and I held a revival in my hometown,

Reuben came with Millie to one of the services.

Reuben had a saliva problem that caused his mouth to be dry. As he gave his life to Jesus Christ that night, not only did he receive salvation, but he also received salivation! He was healed. Reuben's wife was faithful to pray and believe God for his salvation. God honored her faith. In their last years, Reuben often testified of what God was doing in his life.

I want to encourage you, don't give up! Reuben had been a drunkard for more than thirty years, but he was saved because of his wife's prayers.

Charles Story, who now heads up Victory's prison outreach, was a tough nut to crack with the gospel. Years ago, his wife Rosemary, started coming to church at Victory Christian Center. She began to learn how to pray and stand in faith for Charles to be born again.

Six weeks after she began praying, Charles came to church on Mother's Day and gave his life to Jesus Christ. Today, he is the only minister who is allowed to go on death row in the McAlester, Oklahoma, prison and hold services each week for the prisoners.

I want to encourage you to be a witness. Sow the seed of witnessing in someone else in the same way you expect someone to witness to your loved ones. Y.ou may not see the fruit of your efforts immediately, but if you hold fast to the confession of your faith, the seed of the Word will work on them.

Years ago at about 11:00 at night, I was reading and the Lord quickened me to go talk to a neighbor down the street. We hadn't lived in that area very long, so I thought, *I'll go talk to him tomorrow.* The Lord said, "You need to go talk to him tonight." So I went down the street and knocked on his door. It took a little while for him to answer, but he came out in a T-shirt and jeans said, "Yeah, what do you want?"

I said, "Are you saved?" That's not exactly how they teach

you to approach people in the Evangelism Explosion class, but it worked. He looked at me very seriously. I explained, "Have you accepted Jesus as your Lord and Savior?" He was what most people would call "a good old boy."

He said, "Yes, I believe in Jesus Christ." I said, "Well, the Lord told me to come over and make sure."

When I was walking away, I asked, "Lord, what was it?" He said, "He has believed, but he needed to declare it and confess it publicly."

Only a short time after that, while he and his wife were on an outing, he died very suddenly of a heart attack. The Lord affirmed to me that I had done the right thing in witnessing to him.

Some people will mock and laugh when you witness to them, but remember, you are an answer to somebody's prayers. What you sow in prayer, you will reap back in your own life.

Praise God!

The big question most people have when you talk about praying someone into heaven is, "They have a will of their own." Don't you think God knows they have a will of their own? Why would He say, "Pray for laborers," if He knows they have a will of their own? It's very simple. God is in the will-changing business! When you were born again, you had your will changed from darkness to light. Even as good as Nicodemus was, Jesus said, **"You must be born again"** (John 3:7). That requires a decision. The point is, God can work on a person's will, so get your mind off of their will and onto God's will. Let God deal with their will. People can get hung up on the issue of another person's will to the point that they won't even pray for the lost.

Ginger Carnes Ullum, former bartender, had her will changed because of the prayers of her parents.

Ginger shares her story:

"I ran from God for nearly seventeen years. I had been raised in a Christian home, although we didn't have a lot of scriptural knowledge. I moved out on my own when I was seventeen when my parents moved to Texas because of my dad's job.

"I was doing a lot of things I knew were wrong, but I shoved it under the rug and never thought about it. When you are a teenager or you are in your early or mid-twenties, unless you have made a genuine commitment to Jesus Christ, usually you are living fast and you don't think about dying tomorrow. You simply don't think about eternity.

"At my daytime construction job, I smoked cigarettes and wore hard-hats and shoes with steel toes. At night I was a bartender. I drank and continued to run from God because I thought to live for Him would mean that I would lose all of my acquaintances. I thought I couldn't have fun. The devil will try to blind the eyes of your understanding, even if you have been raised in a Christian home.

"When I talked to my parents on the phone, I felt like my dad had a video camera. I thought he knew everything I was doing.

"I would turn on the TV and someone would be preaching.

"The last two months before I came to the Lord, He planted my dad in my home for a month. My parents were getting ready to move back to Tulsa, and Dad needed to be in Tulsa during the week. He stayed in my home on a rollaway bed in the front room.

"I had to keep the smoke out of the house, hide all the liquor and dust myself off, so to speak, before I came home at night. I would wait until bedtime to go home, and I was barely able to open the door and tiptoe past my dad. My dad just prayed for me and loved me.

"After Dad spent a month with me, I started reading the Word again. I began listening to some Christian tapes.

"I went to Victory Christian Center three Sundays in a row, and on the third Sunday, I bellied up to the altar as I had done in the bars for years. I was delivered from drugs, alcohol and sinful living.

"I had no idea my parents were in the service at Victory that day, but they had come to hear Kenneth Copeland, the special speaker. My mother called me that afternoon and said, 'Ginger, I was there when you received Christ today.' They got to see some of the fruit of their labor of years of prayer for me."

Jesus Is the Answer!

Jesus is the Answer to every need. He delivers, saves, heals and restores, regardless of a person's past. True repentance and a genuine salvation experience will cause you to **"go and sin no more"** (John 8:11).

Sinners have not believed because they have been blinded to the truth, or they have not heard a bold witness of the truth. It's time to pray the devil off of their back and the blindness out of their eyes. Pray for Jesus to be lifted up in their midst. Pray for the Spirit of God to convict them, and pray laborers to cross their path every day. Pray that they will get a vision of heaven and hell, realizing that there is an eternal judgment.

I am convinced that the person who really sees Jesus with the devil off his or her back and understands there is a heaven and a hell will be motivated to receive Jesus Christ.

We come into agreement with Your Word, Father, that it is Your will that the lost be saved and come to a knowledge of the truth. We pray that You would be exalted in their midst, Lord Jesus, drawing them unto You in this hour like a holy magnet! We command the darkness and blindness, deception and delusion to leave them now, in the name of Jesus. Let Your light flood them with a knowledge of Your will in all wisdom and understanding, Lord. Thank You for moving in their lives, in the name of Jesus.

It's time to move from petition to rejoicing, and thank the

Lord for His deliverance and salvation of the people for whom you have been praying.

Gospel Prayer Truths

Here are seventeen gospel prayer truths from Chapter 14:

1. Because God's Word never changes (Matthew 24:35), when we base our prayers on His promises, we will receive His answers.

2. As a born-again believer, God promises that your household will also be saved (Acts 16:31).

3. There will be an everlasting fire in hell for those who reject Jesus Christ.

4. God's desire is that all men be saved and come to a knowledge of the truth (1 Timothy 2:4).

5. It is Satan, the god of this world, who blinds the minds of unbelievers to the truth of Jesus Christ.

6. Man's failures do not change the will of God.

7. You can pray for the eyes of the understanding of unbelievers to be enlightened (Ephesians 1:18).

8. If you will mix faith with God's promises, He will perform them.

9. God promised that the seed of the righteous will be delivered (Proverbs 11:21).

10. In the midst of the world's darkness, God's glory will be seen upon believers (Isaiah 60:2).

11. Unbelievers and kings will be drawn to God's glory that rests upon believers (Isaiah 60:3).

12. **"Go into all the world and preach the gospel to every creature"** (Mark 16:15) is a commission to every believer.

208

13. God's power can break through any bondage of the devil.

14. You can pray for Word-believing laborers to cross the paths of your loved ones and friends (Matthew 9:38).

15. What you sow in prayer, you will reap back in your own life.

16. Although it is true that each person has a will of his or her own, God is in the will-changing business!

17. When genuine repentance and salvation have taken place, the person will **"go and sin no more"** (John 8:11).

QUESTIONS

Part 1. Completion

Please complete each of the statements.

1. Acts 16:31 contains a beautiful promise for household salvation: "Believe on the Lord Jesus Christ, and you will be saved, you and your _____."

2. Seven days before the flood, God spoke to Noah: "Come into the ark, you and all your _____, because I have seen that you are righteous before Me in this generation" (Genesis 7:1).

3. God's will is that _____ men be saved and come to the knowledge of the truth (1 Timothy 2:4).

4. Romans 10:13 says, "_____ calls on the name of the Lord shall be saved."

5. Again in 2 Peter 3:9, God's will is expressed that He is not willing that anyone should _____ but that all would _____.

6. Proverbs 11:21 KJV says, "The seed of the _____ shall be delivered."

7. In soulwinning, you have been given authority as a believer to pray and command the _____ _____ that have held people captive to be removed.

8. It is the _____ _____ Who convicts of sin and reveals Jesus Christ to people. You can pray for a spirit of _____ to be loosed over the lost.

9. Jesus said if He is lifted up, He will draw _____ _____ to Himself (John 12:32). You can pray for Jesus to be lifted up in the earth so sinners will be drawn unto Him.

10. According to Matthew 9:38, you can pray for _____ to cross the paths of those who are lost.

11. We are to follow Jesus' example. Matthew 9:35 says He went about all the cities and villages doing three specific things. Please name them:

    a. _____

    b. _____

    c. _____

12. Please name six items that might serve as a laborer in an unsaved person's life:

    a. _____

    b. _____

    c. _____

    d. _____

    e. _____

    f. _____

13. Pastor Daugherty said that a _____, "The Four Spiritual Laws," served as one of the laborers in his life to bring him into relationship with Christ.

Part 2. Personal Application

Please complete the questions and/or statements to the best of your ability.

1. I am standing on the promise of Acts 16:31 for the salvation of

   _____

   _____

   _____

   _____

2. I am standing in the gap in prayer for the salvation of (other than family members) _____

   _____

   _____

   _____

   _____

3. Of the signs Jesus said would follow believers in Mark 16:15-18, the signs that already have been operational in my life are

   _____

   _____

   _____

   _____

4. In the last month, I have witnessed the fruit of my prayers for salvation in the lives of

   _____

   _____

   _____

   _____

5. In obedience to the steps given in this chapter for praying for someone's salvation, I pray now in Jesus' name for

- The blindness to be removed from _____'s eyes.

- Jesus to be lifted up in _____'s midst.

- A spirit of repentance to be loosed upon _____'s life.

- Laborers to cross _____'s path every day.

- I thank and praise You now, Lord Jesus, for _____'s deliverance and salvation.

213

CHAPTER 15

PRAYER THAT STOPS THE DEVIL

Therefore submit to God. Resist the devil and he will flee from you.

James 4:7

Through Jesus' death, burial and resurrection, you have been given the victory over anything you will ever face. Yet, you must resist the devil in your daily walk, or James would not have mentioned it. The enemy has been conquered, but he still must be resisted.

The way to resist the devil starts with the word *submit*. To submit to God means to surrender to Him, to yield yourself fully to Him, to come under His authority. You can't have authority unless you are under authority. To *submit* means to be a doer of the Word and not just a hearer. It means to believe, speak and obey God's Word. *Submission* could be stated another way: *have faith in God.* Hebrews 11:6 says, **"But without faith it is impossible to please Him, for he who comes to God must believe that He is, and that He is a rewarder of those who diligently seek Him."**

Prayer that stops the devil is based upon believing, speaking and acting upon what God says. Submission is not only to the written Word of God, but it is also to the spoken Word when we are under the Holy Spirit's authority.

There are people who will not submit to God because they don't want to be under His authority. They have failed to realize that if you aren't under God's authority, you are under the devil's authority. There is no middle ground. People who are selfishly-ruled are Satan-ruled.

To *resist* the enemy means an active, willful decision to say "no" to the devil with your heart, mind, words and attitude. Every time you invite the will of God to be done in your life, you are saying "no" to the devil. Every time you praise God, you are saying "no" to the devil. Every time you obey the Word of God, you are saying "no" to the devil. In other words, you are making positive choices that literally evict the enemy! You are choosing the will, purposes and desires of God. When you resist the devil, he will flee from you.

To pray to stop the devil, you must believe in the power of Jesus' blood.

Hebrews 10:16-19 says:

"This is the covenant that I will make with them after those days, says the Lord: I will put My laws into their hearts, and in their minds I will write them,"

Then He adds, "Their sins and their lawless deeds I will remember no more."

Now where there is remission of these, there is no longer an offering for sin.

Therefore, brethren, having boldness to enter the Holiest by the blood of Jesus.

We have boldness, confidence and liberty to enter into the holiest place through the blood of Jesus Christ.

Years ago when Sharon and I were on Richard Roberts' Program, he was interviewing a former satanist witch. She said, "Whenever the blood of Jesus is mentioned, it stops the power of satanists."

It was Jesus' blood that destroyed Satan's hold over you and me. It was His blood that ransomed us from Satan's authority. It was His blood on the cross that bought and paid for our total salvation, so when we come to God, we are coming through the blood of His Son. Every time we quote Romans 8:1, we are declaring the power of Jesus blood: **"There is therefore now no condemnation to those who are in Christ Jesus, who do not walk according to the flesh, but according to the Spirit."**

If you do not believe in the power of Jesus' blood, you will not pray with authority. You will be reminded of what you have done in the past, of your failures and shortcomings, and as a result, your prayers will be like a wet noodle. The devil knows when you don't know your authority. It takes the blood of Jesus to free you of guilt and condemnation. It takes an understanding of the blood of Jesus to know your sins have been remitted.

When you call on the power of Jesus' blood, you have immediate access to the heavenly Father.

To have prayer that stops the devil, you must approach the Father in the name of Jesus.

In John 16:23,24, Jesus said to His disciples in preparation for His departure from them:

> **"And in that day you will ask Me nothing. Most assuredly, I say to you, whatever you ask the Father in My name He will give you.**
>
> **"Until now you have asked nothing in My name. Ask, and you will receive, that your joy may be full."**

God wants you to have fullness of joy. He doesn't want the enemy to overrun your life in any area. The Bible says that the shield of faith quenches every fiery dart of the wicked (Ephesians 6:16). David the Psalmist declared, **"The Lord is my shepherd; I shall not want"** (Psalm 23:1). He said, **"Many are the *afflictions* of the righteous, but the Lord delivers him out of them *all*"** (Psalm 34:19).

First John 5:18 says, **"He who has been born of God keeps himself, and the wicked one does not touch him."**

Psalm 91:10 says, **"No evil shall befall you, nor shall any plague come near your dwelling."** Isaiah 54:17 says, **"No weapon formed against you shall prosper, and every tongue which rises against you in judgment you shall condemn...."** Then, how much place should the devil have in your life? *Absolutely none!*

Jesus already won a victory that is sufficient to give us *complete liberty* from the devil's work in our lives, but we have to enter into the type of prayer that will stop him. That's *believing* prayer in the name of Jesus Christ.

I've heard some people in business say, "If you want to get something done, don't mess around at the lower level. Go straight to the top." I always laugh when someone says that, because when they get to the top, they're still not at the top!! If you want to get something done, why don't you go over the top to the top? *Go to Jesus! Go to the Father in Jesus' name!* That name is above the head of every company. Go to the very top! He has authority, and when you go to the Father in Jesus' name, He will help you and give you the wisdom and the avenue to the provision you need.

Jesus has authority because...

> [He] **made Himself of no reputation, taking the form of a bondservant, and coming in the likeness of men.**
>
> **And being found in appearance as a man, He humbled Himself and became obedient to the point of death, even the death of the cross.**
>
> **Therefore God also has highly exalted Him and given Him the name which is above every name,**
>
> **That at the name of Jesus every knee should bow, of those in heaven, and of those on earth, and of those under the earth,**
>
> **And that every tongue should confess that Jesus**

Christ is Lord, to the glory of God the Father.
Philippians 2:7-11

When we use Jesus' name, we have used the highest name in heaven, on earth and under the earth. There is no other authority greater than the name of Jesus.

You and I have been given the power of attorney to use that name! Jesus was saying to His disciples and to you and me, "I am going away. I will send the Comforter [My Spirit] to you. Carry on business as usual, because I am giving you My name. I will never leave you. I will never abandon you. I will be with you always, to the end of the world."

Several years ago, a female student on the O.R.U. campus stopped an attacker with *the name of Jesus*. His intent was to rape her, but when she used Jesus' name, he fled. A few days later, he turned himself in to authorities because of the impact that name had on him!

To pray to stop the devil, you must declare God's Word. Hebrews 4:12 says:

For the word of God is living and powerful, and sharper than any two-edged sword, piercing even to the division of soul and spirit, and of joints and marrow, and is a discerner of the thoughts and intents of the heart.

Because God's Word is a living entity, you can take it into your prayer closet. This is an aspect of prayer that many people have not entered into because they have not recognized the value of it. They pray, beg and plead, but they never come with the Word. If you will start your prayers with God's will, which is His Word, you will never pray amiss.

If you are approaching God for healing, come into agreement with His promises of healing in Isaiah 53:4,5, Matthew 8:17, and 1 Peter 2:24. You can pray, "Father, I am coming to You through the blood of Jesus, in the name of Jesus and with Your Word. You put sickness and disease upon Your Son, Jesus Christ, so I wouldn't have to bear it. By His stripes I am healed. Thank You for my healing now, in Jesus' name."

In chapter 5, "Praying God's Word," I gave you much more information on the importance of praying God's Word.

Second Peter 3:9 says, **"The Lord is not slack concerning His promise...."** So let's not be slack in possessing His promises. We possess them by believing and speaking God's Word in prayer and then acting as if it is so in our lives, even before the manifestation. Glory to God!

Gospel Prayer Truths

Here are seventeen gospel prayer truths from Chapter 15:

1. You will never have authority unless you are under authority.

2. Although the devil has already been conquered, you must resist him with God's Word.

3. Prayer that stops the devil is based upon believing, speaking and acting upon God's Word.

4. If you aren't under God's authority, you are under the devil's authority.

5. Every time you invite God's will to be done in your life, you praise God, or you obey God's Word, you are saying "no" to the devil.

6. You can make positive choices in life that will literally evict the enemy.

7. When you are submitted to God and you resist the devil with God's Word, the devil has no choice but to flee from you.

8. Prayer that stops the devil is based upon a recognition of the power of Jesus' blood.

9. It is the shed blood of Jesus Christ that ransoms the lost from Satan's authority.

10. To come to God is to come through the blood of His Son, Jesus Christ.

11. You must believe in the power of Jesus' shed blood to pray with authority.

12. Prayer that stops the devil will be directed to the Father in Jesus' name.

13. God promised to deliver the righteous from *all* afflictions (Psalm 34:19).

14. No weapon formed against the righteous will prosper (Isaiah 54:17).

15. Believing prayer made in the name of Jesus Christ will stop the devil.

16. The name of Jesus is above every name that can be named (Philippians 2:9). No authority is greater than the name Jesus.

17. If you pray according to God's Word, you will never pray amiss.

QUESTIONS

Part 1. Completion
Please complete each of the statements.

1. To effectively resist the devil, you must first be _____ to God (James 4:7).

2. To submit to God means to yield yourself fully to His _____.

3. It is impossible to please God without _____ (Hebrews 11:6).

4. The writer of Hebrews says of the person who comes to God, "[He or she] must _____ that He is, and that He is a _____ of those who diligently seek Him" (Hebrews 11:6).

5. People who are not under God's authority are under the _____ authority.

6. To pray to stop the devil, you must believe in the power of Jesus' _____.

7. Because of the power of Jesus' blood, "There is now no condemnation to those who are in Christ Jesus, who do not walk according to the _____, but according to the _____" (Romans 8:1).

8. The _____ of Jesus will free you from guilt and condemnation.

9. To have prayer that stops the devil, you must approach the Father in the name of _____. "_____ you ask the Father in My name He will give you" (John 16:23).

10. "He who has been born of God _____ himself, and the wicked one does not touch him" (1 John 5:18). To *keep* means to stop sinning, allowing Jesus Christ to fully reign in your life. It means to be led by the Spirit rather than by the flesh.

11. Philippians 4:10,11 says, "That at the name of Jesus
_____ _____ should bow, of those in heaven,
and of those on earth, and of those under the earth, and that
_____ _____ should confess that
Jesus Christ is Lord, to the glory of God the Father."
12. Prayer that stops the devil will declare _____
_____.

Part 2. Personal Application
Please complete the questions and/or statements to the best of
your ability.

1. In my life, the shed blood of Jesus means _____

_____

_____

_____

_____

2. In my life, the name of Jesus means _____

_____

_____

_____

_____

3. In my life, the Word of God means _____

_____

_____

_____

_____

CHAPTER 16

BREAKTHROUGHS IN PRAYER

I't's time for prayer breakthroughs! Acts 12 gives a graphic picture of what happens when believers pray and when they don't pray.

Now about that time Herod the king stretched out his hand to harass some from the church.

Then he killed James the brother of John with the sword.

And because he saw that it pleased the Jews, he proceeded further to seize Peter also. Now it was during the Days of Unleavened Bread.

So when he had arrested him, he put him in prison, and delivered him to four squads of soldiers to keep him, intending to bring him before the people after Passover.

Acts 12:1-4

James, the brother of John, one who had left his nets to follow Jesus and was close to Jesus, was killed. Peter was imprisoned. It was very clear that Herod intended to kill Peter just as he had killed James. The anger of the people had been stirred up, and what Herod had done to James pleased the people. But something happened to save Peter's life.

Peter was therefore kept in prison, but constant prayer was offered to God for him by the church.

Acts 12:5

Continual prayer was offered to God by the church in Peter's behalf.

> **And when Herod was about to bring him out, that night Peter was sleeping, bound with two chains between two soldiers; and the guards before the door were keeping the prison.**
>
> **Now behold, an angel of the Lord stood by him....**
>
> **Acts 12:6,7**

Remember, chains and bars can't stop angels! They have access to all places. An angel came and stood right beside Peter.

> **And a light shone in the prison; and he struck Peter on the side and raised him up, saying, "Arise quickly!" And his chains fell off his hands.**
>
> **Then the angel said to him, "Gird yourself and tie on your sandals"; and so he did. And he said to him, "Put on your garment and follow me."**
>
> **So he went out and followed him, and did not know that what was done by the angel was real, but thought he was seeing a vision.**
>
> **When they were past the first and the second guard posts, they came to the iron gate that leads to the city, which opened to them of its own accord....**
>
> **Acts 12:7-10**

Wal Mart didn't have the first electronic doors! God had them ahead of everyone. That gate opened of its own accord.

> **And they went out and went down one street, and immediately the angel departed from him.**
>
> **And when Peter had come to himself, he said, "Now I know for certain that the Lord has sent His angel, and has delivered me from the hand of Herod and from all the expectation of the Jewish people."**
>
> **So, when he had considered this, he came to the**

house of Mary, the mother of John whose surname was Mark, where many were gathered together praying.

And as Peter knocked at the door of the gate, a girl named Rhoda came to answer.

When she recognized Peter's voice, because of her gladness she did not open the gate, but ran in and announced that Peter stood before the gate.

But they said to her, "You are beside yourself!" Yet she kept insisting it was so. So they said, "It is his angel."

Acts 12:10-15

They had the same problem Peter had. While Peter thought it was a vision, they thought it was an angelic vision.

Now Peter continued knocking; and when they opened the door and saw him, they were astonished.

But motioning to them with his hand to keep silent, he declared to them how the Lord had brought him out of the prison....

Acts 12:16,17

The same spirit that was in Herod is in the world today, and Christians in various parts of the world are targeted, like Peter, to be destroyed. But when believers pray, a *standard is raised up to stop the work of the enemy*. Sickness, calamity, tragedy, divorce, division and execution are stopped when believers pray. We are in a serious time on the earth. This is no hour to take lightly our protection, deliverance and salvation.

James, a mighty warrior of God who could have reached many people on the earth, was taken out early by the enemy's plan.

There are no lost people in heaven to witness to, no demons to cast out, no sick people to be healed. We are in the earth for a holy, divine purpose, and that is to witness of Jesus Christ, the Savior, Healer and Deliverer. We are on the earth to fulfill God's purposes and plans.

227

Jesus said that God's plan for us is good. His plan is for an abundant life, but the devil's plan is to steal, kill and destroy (John 10:10).

My call to you is to stir yourself up in prayer in behalf of other members of the Body of Christ—for people who are in distress and are going through struggles and difficulties or battling a sickness or disease. It's time that we stop the works of darkness. Because constant prayer was offered by the church for Peter, God intervened by sending an angel. There is no clearer picture in Scripture of the effectiveness of fervent prayer. One man was killed early and another was spared. Does that mean God had a better plan for Peter than He had for James? No! Too often people lay the blame of negative situations on the sovereignty of God.

There are a few holes in that position. One of them is that God did not have a plan for Adam and Eve to disobey Him in the Garden, but God gave man a free will. Saul disobeyed and Judas betrayed the Lord, but they each acted out of their own free will.

John Wesley said that it seems God will do nothing except someone prays. God made the earth, put man in it and gave us authority in Jesus' name to dominate the earth. Adam and Eve sold out to Satan. History has proven the devil's nature, which is to steal, kill and destroy.

When Jesus came, He destroyed the devil's power and regained the dominion that was lost. To all who will believe in Jesus Christ, make Him Lord, put on the helmet of salvation, the breastplate of righteousness, gird up their loins with truth, put the Good News of peace on their feet, take the shield of faith and the sword of the Spirit (the Word of God) and begin to pray in the Spirit, they can stop the devil's will from being done.

Why would Jesus teach us to pray, **"Your kingdom come. Your will be done on earth as it is in heaven"** (Matthew 6:10) if the will of God automatically is done? Why would we pray this if everything that is going to happen is God's will? A lot of junk is going on in the world which is not the will of God.

It's not the will of God that people go home prematurely. Some people have missed God's plan for their lives. God sovereignly chose to give man free will, and He has sovereignly chosen to work through the faith of people who believe Him. That's why Jesus could say to sick people who received His healing virtue, "Your faith has made you whole." Many people could have touched Jesus and received their healing, but only those who turned their faith loose received of Him.

God has a plan for your life. Early morning prayer, prayer in the day time and prayer in the evening time are essential to make sure that His plan is fulfilled in your life.

If your life is not anchored in Jesus Christ through prayer and a relationship with Him, Satan and his forces will attempt to knock you off track, to abort God's plans for you and bring depression, discouragement and defeat.

Constant, fervent prayer will bring you through to victory. When the church rose up in constant prayer for Peter, Satan's plans were stopped.

The Lord has all power and authority, but He has given believers the right to pray and release His power into the earth. Prayer is listening, communing, hearing the voice of the Lord and being built up and strengthened. But there is another aspect to prayer where you declare the will of God to be done with your own words. Remember, His Word and His will are one and the same.

The Word is forever settled in heaven (Psalm 119:89). When you declare, "Lord, Your will be done," then you become the establishing witness on the earth. Jesus has entered into heaven with His blood, and the covenant that has been made for us is forever settled. But you have to make the declaration, "Jesus, You are the Lord of my life, and I will not bow my knee to the devil."

It is established in heaven that Jesus is Lord and that He defeated the devil. Jesus is Lord of heaven, earth and all that is under the earth, but He is not Lord in your life until you declare, "Lord, Your will be done in my life."

It is the same way with healing. It is established in heaven that Jesus bore our sicknesses, carried our diseases and redeemed us from the curse. It is a settled fact, but you have to take an immovable stand on the Word of God and establish it on the earth. God watches over His Word to perform it.

To stand upon the promises of God, you must declare them with your mouth: "Thy will be done on the earth as it is in heaven." How much sickness is in heaven? None! How much sin is in heaven? None! That is God's will on earth—no sickness, no sin, no fear, no torment. He wants the peace, joy, light and life of His Kingdom in the earth, so we have to declare it.

Some people have said, "I've declared it, and it's not working." That's because two things are coming out of your mouth: 1) You are declaring God's Kingdom, and 2) You are declaring that it isn't working. You need to undo the negative and begin to say, "Whether I see it or feel it, God's Word is working in me."

Hebrews 10:23 KJV says, **"Let us hold fast the profession of our faith without wavering; (for he is faithful that promised)."**

James 1:5-8 says:

> **If any of you lacks wisdom, let him ask of God, who gives to all liberally and without reproach, and it will be given to him.**
>
> **But let him ask in faith, with no doubting, for he who doubts is like a wave of the sea driven and tossed by the wind.**
>
> **For let not that man suppose that he will receive anything from the Lord;**

He is a double-minded man, unstable in all his ways.

The reverse of verse 8 also is true: A single-minded person is stable in all of his, or her, ways and will receive whatever he, or she, asks of the Lord.

James 5:14,15 says:

Is anyone among you sick? Let him call for the elders of the church, and let them pray over him, anointing him with oil in the name of the Lord.

And the prayer of faith will save the sick, and the Lord will raise him up. And if he has committed sins, he will be forgiven.

Notice, it's not the prayer of doubt, the prayer of wishing, or the remembrance prayers that are effective. The prayer of faith is based on the written Word of God. Someone who knows the promises of God, lays claim to them, prays and believes he, or she, receives the moment prayer is offered, will receive of the Lord.

Simply defined, the prayer of faith is Mark 11:24: **"Whatever things you ask when you pray, believe that you receive them, and you will have them."** Believe you receive when you pray—not when you see it or feel it.

The other part of the definition of the prayer of faith is found in 1 John 5:14,15:

Now this is the confidence that we have in Him, that if we ask anything according to His will, He hears us.

And if we know that He hears us, whatever we ask, we know that we have the petitions that we have asked of Him.

To ask according to God's will is to pray the promises of His Word. Pray what God has already spoken and written. You can find the promises of God on any subject from childbirth to dying, to believing God for the salvation of loved ones, to strength and wisdom. Every area that relates to your life is covered in His Word.

In James 5:14,15, it is evident that forgiveness and healing come together through the prayer of faith. Then James says, **"Confess your trespasses to one another, and *pray for one another*, that you may be healed..."** (v. 16).

In our services at Victory Christian Center, many people are healed as they pray for someone else. What you give out will come back to you. When you bless someone else, God's blessings will come back to you.

"The effective, fervent prayer of a righteous man avails much" (v. 16). *The Living Bible* says, **"The earnest prayer of a righteous man has great power and wonderful results."** James is talking about heartfelt, genuine, sincere prayers that make great power available in the earth. If we ever needed great power, it is in this hour.

If you have been made righteous by the blood of Jesus Christ, the devil wants to tell you that your prayers don't count. But your prayers have as much power with God as the most well-known Christian speaker in the world. Why? Because we gain access to God by the blood of Jesus Christ, not by great talents and abilities.

Anyone made right by the blood of Jesus Christ makes great power available. How great is it? Great enough to send an angel into a prison and loose a person guarded by dozens of soldiers!

That means with God's power we can bring someone out of a coma and off of a death bed. That means it could deliver someone when a thief tries to break into their house.

Constant prayer was made to God for Peter by the church, and God sent His angel to deliver him. God still has angels available to bring answers to our prayers.

There is an invisible release of the light of God the moment we pray. As we pray, an angel could be ten thousand miles away delivering a missionary.

Matthew 21:22 says, **"And whatever things you ask in prayer, believing, you will receive."** When you know something is God's will, then you can have faith to believe it.

There is something about God—He likes His own ideas! You can pray over your own ideas for a long time, but you get one little idea from Him and you won't have to pray very long before you see a breakthrough!

Gospel Prayer Truths

Here are ten gospel prayer truths from Chapter 16:

1. Constant prayer offered to God on anyone's behalf will stop the devil's schemes.

2. God's angels are never restricted by natural barriers.

3. When believers pray, a standard is raised up to stop the work of the devil.

4. Believers are on the earth to fulfill God's plans and purposes.

5. The works of darkness can be stopped through constant, fervent prayer.

6. God has given believers the right to pray and release His power into the earth.

7. You cannot waver in believing and confessing the promises of God and expect to receive of the Lord.

8. The prayer of faith is based on the written Word of God.

9. You should believe you receive the moment you pray (Mark 11:24).

10. What you give out in prayer will come back to you.

QUESTIONS

Part 1. Completion

Please complete each of the statements.

1. In Acts 12 we find the account of James being killed by Herod. Because it pleased the people, Herod planned to kill Peter, too. A divine intervention was made for Peter, because "constant _____ was offered to God for him by the church" (v. 5).

2. When people pray, a _____ is raised to stop the work of the enemy.

3. While the devil's purpose is to steal, kill and destroy, God's plan for you is for _____ life.

4. Psalm 119:89 says God's _____ is forever settled in heaven.

5. The writer of Hebrews admonishes us to "hold fast the profession of our faith without wavering; (for he is _____ that promised)" (Hebrews 10:23 KJV).

6. James says the double-minded person is _____ in all of his or her ways (James 1:8). The single-minded person then is _____ in all of his or her ways.

7. James 5:15 contains a beautiful promise for a breakthrough in your physical and spiritual well-being: "And the prayer of _____ (believing and speaking God's Word) will save the sick and the Lord will raise him up. And if he has committed sins, he will be forgiven."

8. The prayer of faith is based on God's _____.

9. First John 5:14,15 assures us that if we will pray according to God's _____ (which is His Word), not only does He hear us, but "we have the _____ we have asked of Him."

10. James brings forgiveness and healing together through the prayer of faith. "Confess your _____ to one another, and pray for one another, that you may be _____" (James 5:16).

11. James 5:16 in *The Living Bible* says, "The earnest prayer of a righteous man has great _____ and wonderful _____."

12. We gain access to the Father in prayer through the _____ of Jesus Christ rather than through great talents and abilities.

13. Praying God's _____ is one of your greatest keys to breakthroughs in prayer.

Part 2. Personal Application

Please complete the questions and/or statements to the best of your ability.

1. I experienced what I believe to be angelic intervention when

_____

_____

_____

_____

_____

2. God's primary purpose for my life is _____

_____

_____

_____

_____

_____

3. To develop my prayer life so my prayers "avail much," I am

_____

_____

_____

_____

_____

_____

_____

_____

CHAPTER 17
SPEAK TO YOUR MOUNTAINS

ow is the time to speak the Word of God to the mountains in your life and see them removed—whether it is a mountain of sickness, lack, division, torment, oppression, or some other challenge.

On one of Jesus' final trips over the Mount of Olives before His betrayal and crucifixion, He taught His disciples:

> Now the next day, when they had come out from Bethany, He was hungry.
>
> And seeing from afar a fig tree having leaves, He went to see if perhaps He would find something on it. When He came to it, He found nothing but leaves, for it was not the season for figs.
>
> In response Jesus said to it, "Let no one eat fruit from you ever again." And His disciples heard it.
>
> So they came to Jerusalem. Then Jesus went into the temple and began to drive out those who bought and sold in the temple, and overturned the tables of the money changers and the seats of those who sold doves.
>
> And He would not allow anyone to carry wares through the temple.
>
> Then He taught, saying to them, "Is it not written, 'My house shall be called a house of prayer for all nations'? But you have made it a 'den for thieves.'"

And the scribes and chief priests heard it and
sought how they might destroy Him; for they
feared Him, because all the people were astonished
at His teaching.

When the evening had come, He went out of
the city.

Mark 11:12-19

Jesus and His disciples left Jerusalem on the same route they
had taken into Jerusalem, up over the Mount of Olives, down to
the little town of Bethany. He taught, ministered and spoke each
day in the temple.

Now in the morning, as they passed by, they
saw the fig tree dried up from the roots.

And Peter, remembering, said to Him, "Rabbi,
look! The fig tree which You cursed has withered
away."

So Jesus answered and said to them, "Have faith
in God.

"For assuredly, I say to you, whoever says to
this mountain, 'Be removed and be cast into the
sea,' and does not doubt in his heart, but believes
that those things he says will be done, he will have
whatever he says.

"Therefore I say to you, whatever things you
ask when you pray, believe that you receive them,
and you will have them.

"And whenever you stand praying, if you
have anything against anyone, forgive him, that
your Father in heaven may also forgive you your
trespasses.

"But if you do not forgive, neither will your
Father in heaven forgive your trespasses."

Mark 11:20-26

There are many wonderful thoughts from this passage of scripture. Often overlooked is the parallel between the fig tree and the nation of Israel. Jesus came to the fig tree, and it was supposed to be bearing fruit. It wasn't so He spoke to it and it withered.

Jesus came to the nation of Israel, and it was supposed to be bearing fruit—the fruit of a righteous, holy nation. He came to the temple and found it a den of thieves. What He had done to the fig tree, He did in the temple. He overthrew the money changers and spoke to them that their house would be left desolate.

It was only a few years later, 70 A.D., after Jesus had spoken it, that the Roman general Titus surrounded the city of Jerusalem and destroyed it.

In Scripture, we are likened to trees. The trees of the field shall clap their hands (Isaiah 55:12). Jesus is the Vine, and we are the branches (John 15:5). He is looking for fruit in our lives—the fruit of answered prayer, the fruit of souls being won to Christ, the fruit of the Spirit of love, joy, peace, longsuffering, kindness, goodness, faithfulness, gentleness and self-control.

On one occasion when this parable was told, the landowner said, "Let's destroy the tree." Then the word came, "No, give it one more year. Let's dig around it, fertilize it and see if it brings forth fruit." Thank God, He is merciful!

Jesus left us an example that we are to follow. He left us a pattern of faith. In verse 14, He spoke to the tree, and the disciples heard it. In other words, it wasn't one of those whisper things. He spoke out loud. Nothing happened visibly at that moment. As you release your faith, nothing may happen visibly at that very moment.

But when Jesus returned by this same route some 24 hours later, the fig tree had dried up from the roots. In the natural, it is impossible for something to dry up that quickly.

Then Jesus commanded, **"Have faith in God."** Romans 12:3 says, **"God has dealt to each one a measure of faith."**

Romans 10:17 says, **"So then faith comes by hearing, and hearing by the word of God."** Hebrews 11:6 says, **"But without faith it is impossible to please Him, for he who comes to God must believe that He is, and that He is a rewarder of those who diligently seek Him."** Hebrews 11:1 says, **"Now faith is the substance of things hoped for, the evidence of things not seen."**

It has been said, "Faith is the title deed to that which is invisible." Corrie ten Boom said, "Faith is the radar that sees through the fog." Thank God for Holy Ghost radar! Faith sees things and catches an image of them, even though they may be beyond natural sight. The image of it is imprinted in us by the Word of God.

Then Jesus said, **"For assuredly, I say to you, whoever says to this mountain..."** (Mark 11:23). Jesus was using the terminology of speaking to a mountain as a figure of speech, saying, "If you have a problem, a difficulty, an obstacle that is like a mountain, you can speak to it to be removed."

Jesus was saying that you can speak to any mountain-size problem to be removed and it has to go. Maybe your mountain is sickness or disease, depression, discouragement, fear, dismay, or financial lack.

Many people talk about their mountain, discuss their mountain and even evaluate their mountain. They take samples of their mountain and compare it with other people's mountains. Then there are mountain conferences or dialogues where people get together and discuss their mountains! There are mountain therapy sessions where everybody brings their mountains together.

Jesus didn't say that we are to discuss our challenges. He said, *"Speak to them!"* He was saying, "Speak directly to your mountains." Speak to cancer. Speak to financial lack. Speak to the rebellion in a child. Speak to the animosity in a situation.

How do we get to the point where we believe that what we say will come to pass and that when we speak to our mountain, it will be removed? Jesus said **"If you abide in Me, and My words abide in you, you will ask what you desire, and it shall be done for you"** (John 15:7).

One of the primary keys to your confidence in prayer is to know that what you are speaking is the will or Word of God.

God said to Joshua:

> **This Book of the Law shall not depart from your mouth, but you shall meditate in it day and night, that you may observe to do according to all that is written in it. For then you will make your way prosperous, and then you will have good success.**
>
> **Joshua 1:8**

If you are going to speak against sickness and disease, you need to settle it in your heart that sickness and disease are not from God. One of the reasons people don't get miracles when they speak is they aren't fully convinced that God didn't give it to them. You must understand which side God is on. Faith that is based upon God's Word will work in speaking to your mountains.

Some people have let their mouth run in every direction. They say any old thing they think. They give everybody a piece of their mind until they have no peace! Their words are out of control, and idle words are spoken. If you are going to speak to your mountains and see them removed, then you will have to get control of your tongue. Your tongue has the power of life and death in it (Proverbs 18:21). You can be snared by the words of your own mouth (Proverbs 6:2).

When Sharon and I first heard about the importance of our words, we agreed to help each other watch our words. You might want to do this with a friend or a family member.

Some of the negative things people say are, "I am afraid I am coming down with a fever." When you have someone helping to watch your words and they say, "I agree with you," you will

241

realize, "I didn't mean it that way." If you didn't mean it, why did you say it?

Faith is a force that aligns your spirit, soul and body with God's Word. When you speak God's Word, there is a release of mighty power.

If you can't say anything positive and full of faith, save your words. No matter what the circumstances are, refuse to bow the knee of your confession to the lies of the enemy.

David heard the giant Goliath, "I am going to feed you to the birds of the air." David had been meditating day and night out on the fields while caring for his father's sheep. He knew his covenant with God. He had been singing the songs of the Lord, and out of his spirit came a rock before the rock ever left the sling! The rock of God's Word was hurled at Goliath. Remember, the little rock in his sling followed the path of the rock that had already come from his lips.

The miracle of finances released into your life will follow the path of the Word that you have already spoken. Healing in your body will follow the path of the Word and the faith that have been released from your lips. David countered the fear that was spoken to him from Goliath with the Word of God.

> **Then David said to the Philistine, "You come to me with a sword, with a spear, and with a javelin. But I come to you in the name of the Lord of hosts, the God of the armies of Israel, whom you have defied.**
>
> **"This day the Lord will deliver you into my hand, and I will strike you and take your head from you. And this day I will give the carcasses of the camp of the Philistines to the birds of the air and the wild beasts of the earth, that all the earth may know that there is a God in Israel.**
>
> **"Then all this assembly shall know that the Lord does not save with sword and spear; for the**

battle is the Lord's, and He will give you into our hands."

1 Samuel 17:45-47

David's words were backed up by Almighty God. When the devil speaks a word and you respond to it with God's Word, there is an immediate encounter.

God's blessings are greater than the curses of the enemy. The life that is in you is greater than the darkness that is in the world. The word of healing that you speak is greater than cancer. It is greater than the sickness or disease that tries to come against you. The word of God's blessing is greater than the word of lack and poverty. *Respond to your giants of challenge with God's Word!*

The conditions you must meet to receive God's blessings are that you *not doubt* in your heart but *believe* that what you say (or pray in line with God's Word) will come to pass. **"Therefore I say to you, whatever things you ask when you pray, believe that you receive them, and you will have them"** (Mark 11:24). If you believe everything you say will come to pass, it will shorten your conversation!

Faith is more than a formula. It is a relationship with God. It is a desire to bring God's will into the earth. When you decree a thing by the Word of God, He will bring it to pass (Job 22:28).

This kind of mountain-moving faith will not work in an atmosphere of unforgiveness, but it will work in an atmosphere of God's love. You can confess until you are blue in the face, but if you are bitter with your sister-in-law, mother-in-law, Grandma, or anyone else, it will not work. If there is a blockage because of unforgiveness, there will be a blockage in God's provision.

In Mark 11:25,26, Jesus said:

"And whenever you stand praying, if you have anything against anyone, forgive him, that your Father in heaven may also forgive you your trespasses.

243

> **"But if you do not forgive, neither will your Father in heaven forgive your trespasses."**

Jesus put the entire faith principle in context: *Believe that you receive when you pray.* Speak out of a heart that is filled with the love of God and keep yourself free of unforgiveness.

Why Does Faith Work?

Your position in faith will affect your position in prayer. From the creation of man in the very beginning, God planned for authority and dominion to be released with words. Everything He spoke was with authority. God made man in His image and likeness (Genesis 1:26,27).

Hebrews 11:3 says, **"By faith we understand that the worlds were framed by the word of God...."** God spoke, "Light, be," and light was. It was the original Word Explosion! Hallelujah! It wasn't a chance bang in the atmosphere. A well-ordered, well-planned bang was released when God's Word was spoken.

We aren't going to create another universe, but from our lips we can speak the very promises and blessings that God has put in His Word. When you begin to pray, "Lord, Your will be done in my life on earth as it is in heaven," the will of God will be done in your life. When you pray, "The path of the righteous is like the light of dawn, which grows brighter and brighter," every bit of darkness has to move out of your pathway.

As you begin to say, "My body is healed by the stripes of Jesus. Sickness and disease, depart from me," the power of God's Word is released. Sickness is shattered, darkness goes and you will walk in health, in Jesus' name. As you command weariness and oppression to leave your life, you will be flooded with God's strength.

Begin to pray the Word over your children: *"You are anointed. You are blessed. You will serve the Lord all the days of your life."* Don't let a negative word come out of your mouth toward your children. If you have spoken negative words, repent and speak God's Word over them.

Continue to pray the Word: *"All of my children are taught of the Lord. They are far from oppression. Fear will not come near them. The seed of the righteous is delivered. No iniquity, uncleanness, rebellion, defilement, or perversion can come into my children, in Jesus' name."*

The power of the laws of faith that God gave in His Word was meant to be applied to everything that our hands touch. We were meant to walk in dominion like Adam and Eve did in the beginning, not to rule with arrogance and oppression, but to rule with the love of God.

What comes out of your mouth in prayer and confession will set the course of your destiny.

In John 14:12-14, Jesus said:

"He who believes in Me, the works that I do he will do also; and greater works than these he will do, because I go to My Father.

"And whatever you ask in My name, that I will do, that the Father may be glorified in the Son.

"If you ask anything in My name, I will do it."

This is the day and the hour for God's people to do great exploits because we are in covenant relationship with Him— speaking His Word, praying His Word and obeying His Word.

Gospel Prayer Truths

Here are eighteen gospel prayer truths from Chapter 17:

1. The words of your mouth contain great power, for good or for evil.

2. Believe that you receive when you pray.

3. An unforgiving heart will block your answers to prayer.

245

4. Jesus is looking for the fruit of answered prayer in our lives.

5. Jesus is looking for the fruit of souls being brought into His Kingdom through our lives.

6. Jesus is looking for the fruit of the Holy Spirit to bear fruit in our lives—love, joy, peace, longsuffering, kindness, goodness, faithfulness, gentleness and self-control.

7. Every person has been given a measure of faith (Romans 12:3).

8. Faith is built as you hear the Word of God repeatedly (Romans 10:17).

9. It is impossible to please God without faith (Hebrews 11:6).

10. Jesus gave us an example of speaking to the natural mountains of challenge and difficulty, causing them to be removed (Mark 11:23).

11. You can have confidence in prayer when you pray the will of God, which is the Word of God.

12. To *meditate* upon God's Word day and night and to *obey* it will make your way prosperous and successful (Joshua 1:8).

13. Faith that is based upon God's Word will work in speaking to your mountains.

14. Your tongue has the power of life and death in it (Proverbs 18:21).

15. You can be snared by the words of your own mouth (Proverbs 6:2).

16. You can hurl the rock of God's Word at your giants and watch them be removed!

17. Your position in faith affects your position in prayer.

18. What comes out of your mouth in prayer and confession will set the course of your destiny.

246

QUESTIONS

Part 1. Completion

Please complete each of the statements.

1. An example of speaking to your mountains is when Jesus spoke to the unproductive fig tree: "Let no one eat fruit from you _____" (Mark 11:14). A few hours later, "the fig tree was _____ _____from the roots" (v. 20).

2. In Mark 11:24, Jesus is saying to believers to "speak" to the mountains of challenge in their lives, and if they do not _____ in their heart, but believe, they will _____ what they have spoken.

3. Mark 11:25,26 identifies _____ as a major hindrance to effective prayer.

4. Every person has been given a measure of _____ (Romans 12:3).

5. Jesus gave a "key" to mountain-moving faith in John 15:7: "If you _____ in Me, and My words _____ in you, you will ask what you desire, and it shall be done for you."

6. The "key" God gave to Joshua (and to you and me) for success and prosperity was to _____in His Word day and night.

7. In your tongue is the power of _____ and _____ (Proverbs 18:21).

8. Proverbs 6:2 says you can be _____ with the words of your own mouth.

9. _____ is a force that aligns your total being— spirit, soul and body—with God's Word.

10. Faith is more than a formula. It is a _____ with God.

11. From the beginning of creation, God planned for authority and dominion to be released with _____.

12. Hebrews 11:3 says that the worlds were framed by faith in the _____ of God.

Part 2. Personal Application

Please complete the questions and/or statements to the best of your ability.

1. The mountain(s) I am presently facing in my life is (are):

_____

_____

_____

_____

_____

2. The fruit being produced through my life right now is

_____

_____

_____

_____

_____

_____

3. What are you doing personally to develop the words "of life," as opposed to negative, death words, from your own mouth?

_____

_____

_____

_____

_____

_____

4. This is my day to perform great exploits for God because

_____

_____

_____

_____

_____

_____

CHAPTER 18

FINISHING THE RACE ON
A TRACK OF PRAYER

The prayer Jesus prayed before His betrayal and crucifixion is an example for us to follow. Jesus revealed to His disciples that He was going to leave and send another Comforter, the Holy Spirit.

Jesus briefly explained the function of the Holy Spirit to the disciples:

> **"But the Helper, the Holy Spirit, whom the Father will send in My name, He will teach you all things, and bring to your remembrance all things that I said to you."**
>
> **John 14:26**

> **"Nevertheless I tell you the truth. It is to your advantage that I go away; for if I do not go away, the Helper will not come to you; but if I depart, I will send Him to you.**
>
> **"And when He has come, He will convict the world of sin, and of righteousness, and of judgment...**
>
> **"When He, the Spirit of truth, has come, He will guide you into all truth; for He will not speak on His own authority, but whatever He hears He will speak; and He will tell you things to come.**
>
> **"He will glorify Me, for He will take of what is Mine and declare it to you...**

"These things I have spoken to you, that in Me
you may have peace. In the world you will have
tribulation; but be of good cheer, I have overcome
the world."

John 16:7,8,13,14,33

Thank God we can have peace in a troubled world. We think
we're in a troubled time now. Imagine how the disciples must
have felt when their Savior was rejected, criticized, ridiculed,
crucified and buried.

Jesus said there would be peace for His children in the midst
of the tribulation and trials that are in the world. We do not deny
that there are tribulations and trials, but *we do deny the right of the
tribulations and trials of the world to be in us!*

Jesus was saying, "As you go into the world, people will
reject you and fight against you like they fought against Me.
There will be obstacles you will face as you preach the gospel to
the world. If they rejected Me, they will reject you, but I have
given you My Word and My Spirit."

**Jesus spoke these words, lifted up His eyes to
heaven, and said: "Father, the hour has come. Glorify
Your Son, that Your Son also may glorify You."**

John 17:1

Jesus asked that the Father be glorified through His life. I
believe that's still a valid prayer. By faith, as we identify with
Jesus' suffering and consider ourselves dead to sin and receive
His resurrection power in us, we can pray, "Father, glorify
Yourself in us, and our lives will glorify You."

**"As You have given Him authority over all flesh,
that He should give eternal life to as many as You
have given Him.**

**"And this is eternal life, that they may know You,
the only true God, and Jesus Christ whom You have
sent."**

John 17:2,3

Eternal life is a very tangible thing. It is the personal, intimate knowing of the Father and of His Son, Jesus Christ. That's why we ask people, "Do you really know Jesus?" The word *know* in the Greek is not like you would know someone whose name is in the paper or like a political candidate, but it's like the knowing that exists between a husband and wife.

Jesus said:

> **"I have glorified You on the earth. I have finished the work which You have given Me to do."**
>
> **John 17:4**

Paul prayed a similar prayer:

> **I have fought the good fight, I have finished the race, I have kept the faith.**
>
> **Finally, there is laid up for me the crown of righteousness, which the Lord, the righteous Judge, will give to me on that Day, and not to me only but also to all who have loved His appearing.**
>
> **2 Timothy 4:7,8**

God has something for each of us to do on the earth. Jesus received His instructions in prayer, and we are to follow His example. The Father imparted into His Son's heart the full vision of all that He was to do on the earth in a time of communion and fellowship. As we run on a track of daily prayer God will show us the things we are to do, too.

> **"And now, O Father, glorify Me together with Yourself, with the glory which I had with You before the world was.**
>
> **"I have manifested Your name to the men whom You have given Me out of the world. They were Yours, You gave them to Me, and they have kept Your word."**
>
> **John 17:5,6**

Our primary goal in life should be to manifest the name of

253

Jesus and the Word of God to the people in this earth. To *manifest* means "to bring forth, to demonstrate, to give out." We should pray, "Lord, help us to manifest Your name in the earth."

"Now they have known that all things which You have given Me are from You."

John 17:7

Jesus goes back to something that happened all during His ministry: He gave the Father credit for what He was saying and for what He was doing. Similarly, we should give God the glory for the things we say and do for His Kingdom.

"For I have given to them the words which You have given Me; and they have received them, and have known surely that I came forth from You; and they have believed that You sent Me.

"I pray for them. I do not pray for the world but for those whom You have given Me, for they are Yours."

John 17:8,9

We are to pray for the people that God gives us to win to Christ. It is our calling to pray for them. We should pray for their eyes to be opened, their ears to be receptive, their minds to be understanding and their hearts to receive the truth. We should pray that the power of the devil be removed from them and the power of God be loosed upon them, so the Lord can work on their will to choose Him and refuse evil.

"And all Mine are Yours, and Yours are Mine, and I am glorified in them.

"Now I am no longer in the world, but these are in the world, and I come to You. Holy Father, keep through Your name those whom You have given Me, that they may be one as We are."

John 17:10,11

To keep means "to guard and protect." Jesus said to keep

them *"that they may be one as We are. "* This should be one of our prayers: "Lord, let there be unity in the Body of Christ. Let there be a joining, a linking, a brotherhood. Let there be a flowing together as one in the Body of Christ, just as You and the Father are one."

> **"While I was with them in the world, I kept them in Your name. Those whom You gave Me I have kept; and none of them is lost except the son of perdition, that the Scripture might be fulfilled."**
>
> **John 17:12**

Jesus was saying, "Father, You gave Me all of them except one, Judas. He is the son of perdition, and he is lost, but all of the others I have kept that the Scripture might be fulfilled."

> **"But now I come to You, and these things I speak in the world, that they may have My joy fulfilled in themselves.**
>
> **"I have given them Your word; and the world has hated them because they are not of the world, just as I am not of the world.**
>
> **"I do not pray that You should take them out of the world, but that** *You should keep them from the evil one."*
>
> **John 17:13-15**

One of the prayers we should pray is, "Lord, keep me, my family and all of Your people from evil. Don't take them out of the world, but keep the evil that's in the world out of each of us."

> **"They are not of the world, just as I am not of the world.**
>
> **"Sanctify them by Your truth. Your word is truth."**
>
> **John 17:16,17**

How are people going to be cleansed and sanctified? Are we going to beat the daylights out of people to take sin out of them?

Blast it out of them? Squeeze them? Jerk them through a knot-hole? I've heard all of those things, but there is only one way to be sanctified, and *it is through the washing of the water of God's Word.*

If hard times could sanctify us, people in certain parts of the world would be sanctified. If pressure, obstacles, disasters and calamities could sanctify people, then the people who have the hardest life would be the sweetest and holiest people of all. But that logic just doesn't fit! Hard times won't necessarily produce sanctification. If a person doesn't pray or get into God's Word, they will become harder with the hard times. It is the Spirit of God Who has to work in our hearts. Our wills have to open up to receive God's truth.

> **"As You sent Me into the world, I also have sent them into the world."**
> **John 17:18**

As Jesus was sent, we are sent. Jesus was sent to destroy the works of the devil. He was sent to seek and to save that which was lost. You and I have been sent into the world for these same reasons.

We have been sent to preach the Good News of the gospel to the poor, to heal the brokenhearted, to preach deliverance to the captives (those bound by Satan and his works), recovery of sight to the blind (both naturally and spiritually) and to set at liberty those who are oppressed (Luke 4:18). We are Jesus' hands extended, His voice speaking and His life flowing in the earth.

We are to be reproducers of the Good News of Jesus Christ that we have heard, not only to make our own lives richer, fuller and better, but to make the lives of others richer, fuller and better, too!

The backbone of our mission is EFFECTIVE PRAYER! Let's begin today to apply the prayer principles contained in this book to our own lives, for only on a consistent track of prayer will we be catapulted into the center of the divine assignment God has for our lives—and complete the race set before us!

Gospel Prayer Truths

Here are six gospel prayer truths from Chapter 18:

1. Though difficulties exist in the world, we can be of good cheer, for Jesus overcame the difficulties for us. In Him we have peace, safety and provision.

2. Pray for God to be glorified in and through your life.

3. You can receive instructions and the full vision for your life in prayer, just as Jesus did.

4. Your primary goal in life should be to manifest the name of Jesus and the Word of God to other people.

5. The only way to be sanctified is through the washing of the water of God's Word.

6. You are a reproducer of the Good News of Jesus Christ in the earth. The backbone of this mission is *prayer*.

QUESTIONS

Part 1. Completion

Please complete each of the statements.

1. In John 14:26 Jesus spoke of two things the Holy Spirit would do for us. Please name them:

   a. _____

   b. _____

2. In John 16:13, Jesus referred to the Holy Spirit as the Spirit of _____, Who would guide us into all _____.

3. It is a valid prayer for every believer to pray, just as Jesus prayed, that the _____ would be glorified in and through our lives.

4. The primary goal of every believer should be to manifest the _____ of Jesus and the _____ of God in the earth.

5. In John 17:17, Jesus prayed that we would be sanctified by God's _____, which is truth. We are to be washed daily with the water of God's Word.

6. We, like Jesus, have been sent into the world to _____ the works of the devil and to bring _____ to those who are lost.

7. According to Luke 4:18, five aspects of our divine commission in this life, as mentioned in this chapter, are to:

   a. _____

   b. _____

   c. _____

   d. _____

   e. _____

258

8. The backbone of every believer's divine mission is
_____   _____.

Part 2. Personal Application

Please complete the questions and/or statements to the best of your ability.

1. My first awareness of the Holy Spirit as a Person with whom I could have a relationship was _____

_____

_____

_____

_____

_____

_____

2. My first experience with the Holy Spirit as a Helper and Comforter was_____

_____

_____

_____

_____

_____

3. The Father will be glorified in my life by _____

_____

_____

_____

_____

_____

4. I arn reproducing the Good News of Jesus Christ in the earth
   by _____

   _____

   _____

   _____

   _____

   _____

APPENDIX 1

DAILY PRAYER JOURNAL

Appendix 1

Daily Prayer Journal

I would suggest that you keep a daily prayer journal, which lists your prayer requests, the dates of your requests, the scriptures upon which you base your requests and the dates when your answers are manifested. It will be an encouragement to your prayer life.

Such a journal might look like the one on the following page. (You may duplicate this form should you wish to do so.)

Daily Prayer Journal

Date	Prayer Request	Scriputre(s) Upon Which You Base Your Request	Date Answer Manifested

For the eyes of the Lord run to and fro
throughout the whole earth,
to shew himself strong in the behalf of
them whose heart is perfect toward him....

2 Chronicles 16:9 KJV

Other Books by
Billy Joe Daugherty

Led by the Spirit

Faith Power

Building Stronger Marriages and Families:
Making Your House a Home

The Demonstration of the Gospel

Killing the Giant of Ministry Debt

You Can Be Healed

Absolute Victory

This New Life

The Power of Your Words

Living in God's Abundance

Heaven Is on Its Feet

Breaking the Chains of Bondage

plus several minibooks

Books by Sharon Daugherty

Avoiding Deception

Called By His Side

Walking in the Fruit of the Spirit

For more information about the ministry
or to receive a product catalog, you may contact:
Victory Christian Center
7700 South Lewis Avenue
Tulsa, OK 74136
(918) 491-7700

Billy Joe and Sharon Daugherty

Billy Joe and his wife, Sharon, minister God's healing, saving and delivering power as a team. Sharon's music, exhortation and prophetic words release the anointing of the Holy Spirit to set people free. Billy Joe preaches and ministers the living Word of victory in Jesus. Signs and wonders follow their ministry.

Billy Joe Daugherty is founder and pastor of Victory Christian Center in Tulsa, Oklahoma, Victory Christian School, Victory Bible Institute and Victory World Missions Training Center. One hundred eighty-four International Victory Bible Institutes have been started in fifty-one countries. He is also founder and CEO of the Tulsa Dream Center, which provides food and clothing distribution, dental/medical clinic, legal counseling, job training, tutoring, and recreation areas. The vision of the Tulsa Dream Center is to see thousands of hurting people restored and empowered to achieve the dream that God has for them.

Other Victory outreaches include taking the Gospel via radio and television in North America, along with shortwave radio and television in other nations, and the distribution of books, tapes and videos. Their four children and sons-in-law work alongside them in the ministry.

Victory Christian Center

267